Collins

Aiming for Level
Reading

5

Caroline Bentley-Davies

Gareth Calway

Nicola Copitch

Steve Eddy

Najoud Ensaff

Matthew Tett

Series editor: Gareth Calway

William Collins' dream of knowledge for all began with the publication of his first book in 1819. A self-educated mill worker, he not only enriched millions of lives, but also founded a flourishing publishing house. Today, staying true to this spirit, Collins books are packed with inspiration, innovation and practical expertise. They place you at the centre of a world of possibility and give you exactly what you need to explore it.

Collins. Freedom to teach.

Published by Collins
An imprint of HarperCollins Publishers
77–85 Fulham Palace Road
Hammersmith
London
W6 8JB

Browse the complete Collins catalogue at
www.collinseducation.com

10 9 8 7 6 5
ISBN 978 0 00 731357 0

Caroline Bentley-Davies, Gareth Calway, Nicola Copitch, Steve Eddy, Najoud Ensaff and Matthew Tett assert their moral rights to be identified as the authors of this work.

British Library Cataloguing in Publication Data.
A Catalogue record for this publication is available from the British Library.

Commissioned by Catherine Martin
Design and typesetting by Jordan Publishing Design
Cover Design by Angela English
Printed and bound in China

With thanks to Sue Chapple, Chris Edge, Mike Gould, Jill Thraves, Gemma Wain and Jo Kemp.

Acknowledgements

The publishers gratefully acknowledge the permissions granted to reproduce the copyright material in this book. While every effort has been made to trace and contact copyright holders, where this has not been possible the publishers will be pleased to make the necessary arrangements at the first opportunity.

Extracts from 'Writing Thrillers for Children' by Anthony Horowitz, reproduced by permission of A&C Black Publishers Ltd. (pp6, 7); 'A Wish for My Children' by Evangeline Paterson, from *Poems to Last a Lifetime*, published by HarperCollins Publishers (p8); 'Nettles' by Vernon Scannell, from *Poems to Last a Lifetime*, published by HarperCollins Publishers (p9); extract from the Vauxhall Meriva 2008 brochure (p10); extracts reproduced by permission of Aston Martin Lagonda (p11); 'A Case of Murder' by Vernon Scannell, from *The Faber Book of Murder*, published by Faber & Faber (pp13, 14); extract from an article in *Daily Mirror* 9 Oct 2008, reprinted by permission of Mirrorpix (p18); extract from an article by Amy Lawrence in *The Observer*, © Guardian News & Media Ltd 2009 (p19); extracts from *Surrender* © 2005 Sonja Hartnett, reproduced by permission of Walker Books, London SE11 5HJ (pp20, 21); extracts from an article by Elizabeth Day in *The Observer*, © Guardian News Media Ltd 2008 (pp22, 23); extracts from Just in Case by Meg Rosoff, reproduced by permission of Penguin Books Ltd. (pp26, 27); back cover blurb from *Breathe* by Cliff McNish, reproduced by permission of Orion Children's Books, London (p30); back cover blurb from *Can You Hear Me* by Penny Kendall, reproduced by permission of Andersen Press Ltd. (p30); extract from *Uglies* by Scott Westerfield, published by Simon & Schuster (p31); extract from an article in *The Sun* 18 December 2008, reprinted by permission of NI Syndication (p32); article by Caroline Sullivan from *The Guardian* © Guardian News & Media Ltd 2009 (p33); article from *Daily Mail*, 13 Oct 2008, reprinted by permission of Solo Syndication (p34); 'Valentine' by Wendy Cope, published by Faber & Faber (p38); 'For the girl crying on the train' by Mike Gould, from *Limited Ballads* by Mike Gould and John Pownall, 2009 (p39); 'Snooker Player' by Richard Freeman, first published in *Ambit Magazine*, 1973 (p43); extract from *Quicksand* by Nella Larsen, published by Rutgers University Press (p44); extracts from *Wolf Brother* by Michelle Paver, reproduced by permission of Orion Children's Books, London (pp46, 47); extract from *Of Mice and Men by John Steinbeck* © John Steinbeck, 1937, 1965, reproduced by permission of Penguin Books Ltd. (p50); illustration by Sonia Leong, from *Manga Shakespeare: Romeo & Juliet* © SelfMade Hero 2007 (p54); extract from *Skeleton Key* © 2005 Anthony Horowitz, published by Walker Books, London SE11 5HJ (p76); extract from *Notes from a Big Country* by Bill Bryson, published by Black Swan (p78); 'The closed school' by Raymond Wilson, from *To Be a Ghost* by Raymond Wilson, published by Viking, part of Penguin Books Ltd. (p80); extract from *Private Peaceful* by Simon Reade, published by Collins Education, part of HarperCollins Publishers (pp82–4); article from *Time* Vol. 173 No.19, 11 May 2009 (p86).

The publishers would like to thank the following for permission to reproduce pictures in these pages.

Advertising Archives (pp72, 73); Alamy (p47); Andersen Press (p30b); army.mod.uk (p71); Corbis (p40); Getty Images (pp8, 20, 23, 33, 61, 67); istockphoto (pp7, 9, 12, 15, 24, 25, 34, 38, 42, 44, 48, 49, 50, 51); Mary Evans Picture Library (p68); Moviestore Collection (p58); mtv.co.uk (p36); Orion Publishing (p30t) PA Photos (p18); Parentline Plus (p56); Photolibrary.com (p26); Rex Features (pp11, 22, 65, 70); Ronald Grant Archive (p32); Simon & Schuster (p31); Vauxhall (p10).

Contents

Chapter 1

AF2 Understand, describe, select or retrieve information, events or ideas from texts and use quotation and reference to text

This chapter is going to show you how to

- Understand and respond to the key points in a text
- Make accurate comments about different parts of a text
- Use quotations and refer to the text to support your ideas
- Comment on the meaning of your quotations.

What's it all about?

Being able to find key points in a text and comment on them effectively.

This lesson will
● help you to identify a writer's key ideas.

When you read a text, you need to ask yourself: what do I understand the main ideas to be? Then ask yourself: what in the text tells me this?

Getting you thinking

Read this extract from an article by Anthony Horowitz.

Writing horror for children

Children love horror. You need look no further than the worldwide success of writers like Darren Shan to see it.

And yet, the first – indeed the most crucial – question you have to ask yourself is: how far can you go? This is something of which I'm always painfully aware. Go into a classroom and talk to the children and you will discover that far enough is never enough. They want the blood, the intestines, the knife cutting through the flesh…

When I visit schools, I always advise children to keep their own writing blood-free. Teachers don't like it, I tell them. I remind them that the scariest moment in any horror film is when the hand reaches for the door handle in the dark. That's when the music jangles and your imagination runs riot. It seems to me that what you imagine will always be scarier than what you see – and this is a rule I apply to my own writing.

1 With a partner, discuss what you think the purpose of this text is and who it is aimed at. Find evidence from the text to support your ideas.

2 Now look at these statements. Which one sums up the writer's key idea? Find evidence in the text that supports your choice.

Children like horror with lots of blood and gore in it.

The best horror stories are those that let the reader imagine the horror.

Successful horror stories are always graphic and violent.

Now you try it

Now read the final part of the article:

My intention has always been to entertain children – by which I mean neither educating them, improving them nor terrorising them. I only ever got it wrong once. I wrote a short horror story where the first letter of each sentence spelled out a message to the reader. That message went something along the lines of: 'As soon as you have read this, I'm coming to your house to kill you.'

About a year later, I received a note from a very angry and distressed mother who told me that she now had a traumatised daughter. My story, she said, was wilfully **irresponsible** and she suggested that I write a letter to her daughter, apologising.

I totally agreed. The next day I wrote a nice letter to the girl, explaining that I had intended to be mischievous rather than **malevolent**, that it was only a story, that she shouldn't have taken it so seriously.

Unfortunately, the first letter of every sentence in my letter spelled out: 'I am going to kill you too.'

- Why did the mother complain?
- Pick out one detail from the text that shows you that Anthony Horowitz didn't take the mother's complaint seriously.

Glossary

irresponsible: not thinking about the consequences of his action

malevolent: wanting or intending to cause harm

Comment on ideas from different parts of a text

This lesson will
● help you to comment on different parts of a poem.

A good reader can pick out **key details** from different parts of a text and **comment** on what they mean.

Getting you thinking

Read this poem and then discuss with a partner what you think it is about.

A Wish for My Children

On this doorstep I stand
year after year
to watch you going

and think: May you not
skin your knees. May you
not catch your fingers
in car doors. May
your hearts not break.

May tide and weather
wait for your coming

and may you grow strong
to break
all the webs of my weaving.

Evangeline Paterson

● Pick out three details in the first two stanzas that tell you about the poet's attitude towards her children.

● Now look at the final stanza. What do you think 'all the webs of my weaving' means?

● Have your ideas about the poet's attitude towards her children changed by the end of the poem?

Now you try it

Read this poem with a partner, then answer the questions below.

Nettles

My son aged three fell in the nettle bed.
'Bed' seemed a curious name for those green spears
That regiment of spite behind the shed:
It was no place for rest. With sobs and tears
The boy came seeking comfort and I saw
White blisters beaded on his tender skin.
We soothed him till his pain was not so raw.
At last he offered us a watery grin,
And then I took my hook and honed the blade
And went outside and slashed in fury with it
Till not a nettle in that fierce parade
Stood upright anymore. Next task: I lit
A funeral pyre to burn the fallen dead.
But in two weeks the busy sun and rain
Had called up tall recruits behind the shed:
My son would often feel sharp wounds again.

Vernon Scannell

- Sum up the events described in the poem in three sentences.
- What are the poet's feelings towards his son? Pick out details that show this.
- What do you think the last line of the poem means?

Remember

Always use quotation marks ('…') to show when you are quoting directly from the text.

Development activity APP

Discuss the similarities and differences in the ideas about parental love that both poems express.

Think about

- the idea of a parent trying to protect their child from harm
- the idea of a parent not being able to protect their child all the time
- children growing up
- any contrasting ideas about being a parent
- how both poems are structured.

Check your progress

LEVEL 4 I can make comments about each poem

LEVEL 5 I can link ideas from different sections of each poem

LEVEL 6 I can compare ideas and comment in detail on both poems

3 Use quotations and refer to the text to support your ideas

This lesson will
- help you to select quotations to support your ideas.

When you are referring to a text, you need to choose **quotations** carefully, making sure you focus only on the part of the text that proves your point.

Getting you thinking

Read this advertisement for the Vauxhall Meriva.

Looking for a compact MPV that's easy to park and manoeuvre around town? A car that makes rear passengers of all ages feel as welcome as those in the front – with adjustable rear seats that fit family members of all sizes and their luggage? Check out the latest Meriva models from Vauxhall. With fresh style, lively engine choices and great features throughout, today's Meriva fits your family's lifestyle – effortlessly.

Stylish. Compact. Spacious. And always fun. With sharp lines and brilliant detailing, the Meriva has bags of visual appeal. And everything is designed to make life that little bit easier, whether you're loading up at the supermarket, finding a place to park or simply heading off for a great day out.

With a partner, pick out quotations from the text that make the Vauxhall Meriva sound

- attractive to look at
- roomy
- a great family car
- powerful.

How does it work?

Once you have found quotations to back up each of these points, you need to think about how to use them in your own writing.

For example, for the first point you might have written down:

attractive to look at	'fresh style'
	'Stylish'
	'sharp lines and brilliant detailing'
	'has bags of visual appeal'

Choose the best short quotation to support the point, and use this in your answer:

> *You get the impression that the Meriva is an attractive car, as the advert says it has 'bags of visual appeal'.*

Now you try it

Now read this advertisement.

> Aston Martin is a name that needs little introduction. It has always stood for high performance sports cars, designed and produced by skilled craftsmen. There is a special place in the market and in the hearts of owners for classic sports cars which conform to this ideal. These are cars which bring to life the freedom and enjoyment of the open road.
>
> Truly great luxury sports cars are few and far between in a world where innovation is all too often hampered by compromise. Designed as the ultimate driving experience, the Aston Martin DBS bridges the gap between road and track. Equally at home on a twisting mountain circuit as on the open road, the DBS is a true thoroughbred.

- With a partner, discuss what sort of person this car advertisement is aimed at. Pick out quotations from the text to support your ideas.
- What does the advertisement suggest are the most important qualities of the Aston Martin? Pick out quotations and refer to the text to support your ideas.

Development activity

Read the two advertisements again.

Write a paragraph recommending which car would be best to buy for

- a young businesswoman with a passion for racing
- a family with three small children.

Remember to include quotations and references to the texts to support your points.

Check your progress

LEVEL 4	I can identify the important factors in the advertisements
LEVEL 5	I can make a recommendation using quotations to support my ideas
LEVEL 6	I can justify my recommendation by analysing quotations from the text

This lesson will
- help you to explain why you have selected quotations and what they mean

A good reader can explain what his or her **quotation means**, and also pick out and comment on individual words in **more detail**.

Getting you thinking

Read this extract from a poem.

> He hated that cat; he watched it sit,
> A buzzing machine of soft black stuff,
> He sat and watched and he hated it,
> Snug in its fur, hot blood in a muff.

Which word do you find most disturbing in this extract?

1 Pick out one word and explain to a partner why you chose this word.

2 Now write out your response to the question.
  You should
  - make your **point**
  - use your quotation (word) as **evidence**
  - **explain** why you chose it and how it makes you feel.

Remember

Keep to this formula for quoting: point, evidence, explanation.

How does it work?

Look at these two student responses. Decide in pairs which student has written most effectively about their quotation.

A *The word that is most disturbing is 'buzzing' because it suggests that the boy is really annoyed by the cat. 'Buzzing' is a word more usually associated with flies and it suggests that he is irritated by the cat. Even the noise the cat makes increases the boy's tension.*

B *The most disturbing thing about the poem is the line: 'he sat and watched and he hated it'. The boy is sitting and watching the cat and he really hates it.*

Now you try it

Here is the opening of the poem. Read it carefully, then copy and complete the table over the page.

A Case of Murder

They should not have left him there alone,
Alone that is except for the cat.
He was only nine, not old enough
To be left alone in a basement flat,
5   Alone, that is, except for the cat.
A dog would have been a different thing,
A big gruff dog with slashing jaws,
But a cat with round eyes mad as gold,
Plump as a cushion with tucked-in paws –
10   Better have left him with a fair-sized rat!
But what they did was leave him with a cat.
He hated that cat; he watched it sit,
A buzzing machine of soft black stuff,
He sat and watched and he hated it,
15   Snug in its fur, hot blood in a muff,
And its mad gold stare and the way it sat
Crooning dark warmth: he loathed all that.
So he took Daddy's stick and he hit the cat.
Then quick as a sudden crack in glass
20   It hissed, black flash, to a hiding place
In the dust and dark beneath the couch,
And he followed the grin on his new-made face,
A wide-eyed, frightened snarl of a grin,
And he took the stick and he thrust it in,
25   Hard and quick in the furry dark.
The black fur squealed and he felt his skin
Prickle with sparks of dry delight.
Then the cat again came into sight,
Shot for the door that wasn't quite shut,
30   But the boy, quick too, slammed fast the door:
The cat, half-through, was cracked like a nut
And the soft black thud was dumped on the floor.

Point	Evidence	Explanation
Lines 1–17 *At the beginning of the poem, we learn that the boy is...* *He feels...*	[Find words or short phrases from the poem that support your point.]	[Explain why you chose these quotations and what they tell you about the boy.]
Lines 18–32 *As the poem continues, we learn more about the boy. We feel that he is really...* *When he attacks the cat he seems...*	[Find words or short phrases from the poem that support your point.]	[Explain why you chose these quotations and what they tell you about the boy.]

- Discuss your word choices with a partner.
- Have you both fully explained the effect of the words you chose?

Development activity

Now read the ending of the poem. Does it end as you expected it to?

Then the boy was suddenly terrified
And he bit his knuckles and cried and cried;
But he had to do something with the dead thing there.
His eyes squeezed beads of salty prayer
But the wound of fear gaped wide and raw;
He dared not touch the thing with his hands
So he fetched a spade and shovelled it
And dumped the load of heavy fur
In the spidery cupboard under the stair
Where it's been for years, and though it died
It's grown in that cupboard and its hot low purr
Grows slowly louder year by year:
There'll not be a corner for the boy to hide
When the cupboard swells and all sides split
And the huge black cat pads out of it.

Vernon Scannell

Try to answer the questions below. For each question, select several short quotations from the poem to support your point and explain why you have chosen them.

- How do you think the boy feels about what he has done?

- Do you think his feelings about killing the cat change as time goes on?

- How does the ending of the poem make you feel?

Check your progress

LEVEL 4   I can express my feelings and use some evidence from the text

LEVEL 5   I can support my ideas with quotations and explanation

LEVEL 6   I can give a convincing opinion, analysing language in detail

Level Booster

LEVEL 4

- I can identify the key pieces of information in a text
- I can select the most important pieces of information
- I can refer to the text itself by picking out quotations

LEVEL 5

- I can select the most relevant pieces of information in a text
- I can read across several texts and pick out the most relevant points
- I can select short, relevant and meaningful quotations
- I can make good and accurate points about a text and support them with my own opinion and a quotation

LEVEL 6

- I can clearly identify the most relevant pieces of information in a text
- I can confidently pick out evidence from a range of texts
- I can select short quotations and discuss their meaning in detail
- I can develop my ideas or a line of argument using quotation to back up my ideas

Chapter 2

AF3 Deduce, infer or interpret information, events or ideas

This chapter is going to show you how to

- Look closely at the meaning of individual words and phrases

- Develop inferences and deductions across a text

- Use quotations effectively to support your inferences and deductions

- Read between the lines according to the purpose of a text

- Make deductions about characters in fiction texts.

What's it all about?

A good reader 'reads between the lines', draws conclusions and develops well-constructed ideas as to what a text is really about. Your ideas must always link very closely to the text and be supported by evidence.

1 Look closely at the meaning of individual words and phrases

This lesson will
- get you thinking about the impact of individual words and phrases.

You need to be able to think about why a writer chooses particular words and phrases. What does the writer's **word choice** add to the meaning of a text?

Getting you thinking

Read this extract from a report of football match.

Rotherham 4–2 Leeds

ROTHERHAM danger man Reuben Reid went crashing down – and Gary McAllister's Leeds went crashing out.

Bristol-born 20-year-old Reid, who abandoned a promising cricket career, hit Leeds for six with a slalom-like run into the penalty area one minute before half-time.

He was felled in desperation.

Daily Mirror (9 October 2008)

With a partner, explain what you think these descriptions mean:
- danger man
- slalom-like run.

What do they suggest about Reuben Reid's footballing skills?

How does it work?

We get the impression that Reuben Reid is a great footballer:
- 'danger man' makes it sound as if he is powerful on the pitch and a real threat to the other team.
- 'slalom-like run' suggests Reid was moving very fast, as slalom is a fast, downhill form of skiing. It implies that he was moving smoothly and gracefully, and was untouchable by other players.

Now you try it

Now read this match report of an FA Cup quarter final between Manchester United and Fulham.

> In search of a greater margin before half-time, Rooney began to sizzle. He chipped a Beckhamesque effort from the centre circle, had one chalked off for offside, dragged another just wide after reading Tevez's sublime pass and then struck a post. So intense was his focus, he did not even look particularly frustrated or bothered not to have scored. Full steam ahead.
>
> United were a goal in front but light years ahead. Besides, it took only another moment for the next goal to come. And what a goal. Tevez sent a 25-yard rocket past Schwarzer and into the top corner of his goal. There were four Fulham defenders in attendance. All looked powerless. One of them, Dickson Etuhu, simply fell over. 'Tevez was a jack-in-the-box all day,' Ferguson said, beaming.
>
> *The Observer* (7 March 2009)

Look closely at the three words below.

sizzle   rocket   sublime

1 With a partner, use a thesaurus to find different words that you could use instead of **powerless** and **rocket**, as has been done here for **sizzle**.

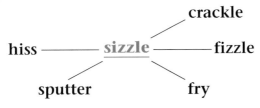

2 Now discuss why you think the writer chose these exact words. What does each word suggest about United's performance?

Remember

Words that have similar meanings are called synonyms.

Top tips

If you are not sure whether a synonym works, double-check its meaning in the dictionary.

Development activity

- With a partner, pick out the words and phrases used to describe Fulham's performance.
- Using a dictionary and a thesaurus, work out the meanings of these words and explain to each other why the writer has chosen them.

Check your progress

LEVEL 4	I can understand the purpose of different words
LEVEL 5	I can explain what certain words and phrases mean
LEVEL 6	I can explain the effect of certain words and phrases

2 Develop your inferences and deductions across a text

This lesson will
- help you to make connections and develop your ideas as you read a novel.

A good reader can **make connections** between different parts of a text. This will help you to work out what a text might mean.

Getting you thinking

Read this extract. It is from the opening chapter of a novel called *Surrender* by Sonya Hartnett.

> Several times a week I must be cleaned. Water comes to me on a sponge. I must lift my arms, shift my heels, lower my flaming eyes. I must smell pink, antiseptic. I'm removed from my place where the bedsheets are changed and set to sag in a wheelchair.

With a partner, discuss what you can **infer** (work out) about the narrator.
- Where do you think the narrator is?
- What do you think has happened to the narrator?

Think about the details given in the text and the clues these give you.

How does it work?

In the opening sentence the narrator states, 'Several times a week I must be cleaned.' This makes the narrator sound like an object or an animal rather than a human being. However, the word 'arms' tells us that this is a person after all. We can deduce that this is a person who is not very happy and feels like an object.

There are clues that suggest the narrator might be in hospital: for instance, when he or she describes being 'set to sag in a wheelchair'.

The suggestion is that the narrator is unable to care for him- or herself at all. Physically, everything must be done for them, yet the narrator's mind is still functioning. So we infer that the narrator is either injured or very ill.

Now you try it

Read the next part of the extract:

> I am **proffered** a pan, and the sight of it shames me; at other times I can't call for it fast enough. My food comes mashed, raised on a spoon; spillage will dapple my lap. I am addressed as if I am an idiot, cooed over as though a child. I'm woken when I wish to sleep, told to sleep when I'd prefer to be awake. I am poked, prodded, pinched and **flensed**, I'm needled and wheedled and **cajoled**.

Glossary

proffered: to be offered something

flensed: to be stripped of something

cajoled: to be encouraged to do something

With a partner, look for clues in this part of the text. What can you deduce about how the narrator feels?

Find and comment on details that tell you

- how the narrator is treated
- what the narrator thinks about this treatment.

Does this passage tell you anything new about the narrator?

Development activity

Now read on:

> My existence is nothing but a series of humiliations, what little life is left to me can hardly be called my own. All of this, this horror, just to say, 'He's dying'.

Remember

It is important to show how your view changes when you get fresh insight into a character or event over the course of a text.

In a small group, read the last sentence again. Discuss what you can infer from this final sentence. Share your ideas with the rest of the class.

Check your progress

LEVEL 4	I can work out some information about the narrator in the story
LEVEL 5	I can find and explain information that backs up my ideas about the narrator
LEVEL 6	I can expand on my ideas to work out what I think is happening in the story

This lesson will
- show you how to use quotations to back up your ideas.

When you are writing about a text, it is important to use **quotations** to back up your ideas. Use PEE to help you present your ideas effectively.

PEE stands for

- **Point:** you make a point about a text
- **Evidence:** you quote from the text to back up your idea
- **Explanation:** you explain why you have chosen it.

Getting you thinking

The text below is taken from a newspaper article about Roald Dahl.

> Part of the reason for Dahl's enduring popularity, says his widow, is that he never spoke down to children: 'They were equals'. This, she thinks, was because he never lost his own sense of childish wonderment.
>
> *The Observer*

- What is interesting about Roald Dahl's popularity? Discuss your ideas with a partner.
- Here are two possible answers to this question. Which one do you think is better?

A
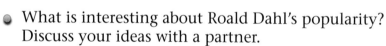
Roald Dahl was popular because he wrote famous books.

B

The article says that Roald Dahl has 'enduring popularity'. This means that his popularity keeps going, it is long lasting. It also says that 'he never spoke down to children'. We can infer that this is why his stories capture the imagination of so many young people.

Now you try it

Now look at this table. Copy and complete the table by explaining what you can infer about Roald Dahl from each quotation from the article. The first one has been done for you.

Quotation	What you can infer from this
Most of us have read his books and had our childhoods shaped by his **fantastical** mind and **macabre** sense of humour.	*Many children have enjoyed Roald Dahl's writing and it has had a big impact on their lives and imaginations.*
He said, 'I feel a bit like a pop star.'	
He would produce pink milk for breakfast or make jelly with hundreds and thousands suspended in the gelatine.	
What makes Dahl's legacy so lasting is his ability to transform the ordinary into something unexpectedly **enchanting**.	

Glossary

fantastical: strange or fanciful

macabre: gruesome

enchanting: magical

Development activity

Here is the poet Michael Rosen's description of meeting Roald Dahl and enjoying his books.

> In every one of the books, he's on the side of the child. He also creates characters that allow children to experience their **conflicted** feelings about adults. I once met Roald Dahl with my oldest son, and he beckoned Joe over and said: 'What's that growing on your father's face? It's a great disgusting growth and it's probably got yesterday's breakfast in it'.

1 Write a paragraph answering these questions:
- What impression do you get of Roald Dahl from this description?
- What does it suggest about why children like Roald Dahl's books so much?

Glossary

conflicted: mixed up

Check your progress

LEVEL 4 I can understand the purpose of using PEE in my writing

LEVEL 5 I can make inferences about Roald Dahl based on different quotations

LEVEL 6 I can write a detailed paragraph explaining what I have deduced about Roald Dahl

4 Read between the lines according to the purpose of a text

This lesson will

● help you to understand different layers of meaning in what you read.

Thinking about the **purpose** of a text will help you to **read between the lines** of what is said.

Getting you thinking

Look at these quotations from estate agent descriptions of properties for sale. In each one the estate agent is trying to describe a feature of the house or flat in a positive way.

Working with a partner, discuss what each quotation might really mean. The first one has been done for you.

Quotation	What it really means
A compact apartment	*It's tiny!*
Would benefit from double glazing	
Internal viewing recommended	
Mature garden	
Would suit DIY enthusiast	
In need of modernisation	

How does it work?

Bear in mind that these phrases are trying to persuade people to buy the house in question. This will help you think about their **real** meaning. For example, 'Would benefit from double glazing' is a way of **not** saying that the house is noisy, cold or poorly insulated. 'Would suit DIY enthusiast' means that the house needs a lot of work!

Remember

Don't always accept the surface meaning but dig deeper to find out what is being implied.

Top tips

Consider the purpose of the text, and try to keep this in mind as you read it.

Now you try it

Read this estate agent's description of Mudlark Cottage.

Mudlark Cottage is a cosy, easy-to-maintain residence which will favour the single person or young couple keen to put their own stamp on a property. With many original features, this is a property which, with a little bit of TLC, can become the perfect starter-home.

The front door opens directly onto the kitchen/diner, thus affording a clear perspective from one end of the house to the other. The current owners are conveniently leaving the stove and washtub, which will no doubt prove useful appliances until more modern fittings can be acquired.

Another interesting feature of the cottage is the link to history with the use of an outside toilet, which is only a few feet away at the end of the garden. The garden itself is easily-maintained due to the concrete that was helpfully laid onto the lawn by the previous owners.

The proximity of the main road directly in front of the house is extremely convenient, and recent safety humps have reduced speeding significantly.

This is the ideal starter home for a single person (or, at a stretch, couple) who doesn't mind a bit of DIY, renovation and in some cases rebuilding work, and enjoys being close to traffic links.

1 With a partner, write down what might be **implied** by each of the following words or phrases:
- 'cosy'
- 'easy-to-maintain'
- 'will favour the single person or young couple keen to put their own stamp on a property'
- 'With many original features'
- 'close to traffic links'.

Development activity **APP**

Now imagine you are working for Floggitt Estate Agents. You have been asked by your boss to rewrite the advert to make the cottage sound more inviting. Your advert should still remain truthful, but **hint** at some of the problems rather than describing them in detail. Remember, you are trying to sell the house!

Check your progress

LEVEL 4	I can understand the different meanings of certain statements
LEVEL 5	I can work out and explain what is implied by certain statements
LEVEL 6	I can apply what I have learned about reading between the lines to my own writing

Make deductions about characters in fiction texts

This lesson will
- help you to develop your understanding of characters' feelings.

It is important to develop your ideas about characters and settings, by reading closely and making inferences.

Getting you thinking

Read this extract from the novel *Just In Case* by Meg Rosoff.

> David Case's baby brother had recently learned to walk but he wasn't what you'd call an expert. He toddled past his brother to the large open window of the older boy's room. There, with a great deal of effort, he pulled himself on to the window sill, scrunched up like a caterpillar, pushed into a crouch and stood, teetering precariously, his gaze fixed solemnly on the church tower a quarter-mile away.

- Note down everything you find out about David's baby brother.

Now you try it

In this next extract from the novel, David spots his baby brother balancing on the window sill.

> In the instant of looking up, David took the measure of the situation, shouted '*Charlie!*' and lunged across the room. He grabbed the child by the cape of his Batman pyjamas, wrapped his arms around him with enough force to flatten his ribs, and sank to the floor, squashing the boy's face into the safe hollow beneath his chin.
>
> Charlie squeaked with outrage, but David barely heard. Panting, he unpinned him, gripping the child at arm's length.
>
> 'What were you doing?' He was shouting. 'What on earth did you think you were doing?'

- What can you infer (work out) about David's feelings towards his brother?

Development activity

Read this final passage from the novel.

> Well, said Charlie, I was bored just playing with my toys and you weren't paying attention to me so I thought I would get a better look at the world. I climbed up on the window which wasn't easy and once I managed to do that I felt strange and happy with nothing but sky all around me and all of a sudden a bird flew past and looked at me and said I could fly and a bird hasn't ever talked to me before and I figured a bird would know what he was talking about when it came to flying so I thought he must be right. Oh, and there was also a pretty grey dog on the pavement who looked up and pointed at me with his nose so I didn't fall and just when I was about to leap out and soar through the air you grabbed me and hurt me a lot which made me very cross and I didn't get a chance to fly even though I'm sure I could have.
>
> The little boy explained all this slowly and carefully, so as not to be misunderstood.
>
> 'Bir-dee fly' were the words that came out of his mouth.

1 With a partner, discuss these questions:
- Do you think Charlie is really speaking in the first paragraph?
- Can David understand what Charlie is saying? How can you tell?
- Why do you think the author includes Charlie's viewpoint like this?

2 Write a short paragraph commenting on what you have discovered about David's and Charlie's relationship in the three extracts.

Remember

Use examples from the text following the PEE structure (point, evidence, explanation).

Check your progress

LEVEL 4 I can work out how a character feels

LEVEL 5 I can work out how a character feels and explain my ideas with evidence from the text

LEVEL 6 I can write a detailed paragraph about two characters' relationship, linking my ideas together

Level Booster

LEVEL 4

- I can understand the purpose of different words in texts
- I can work out what information means in texts
- I can understand why certain words are used to describe events

LEVEL 5

- I can explain what certain words and phrases mean
- I can find and explain required information
- I can make inferences based on quotations that I read
- I can find quotations to back up my ideas

LEVEL 6

- I can make choices about the most effective words and phrases to use in my writing
- I can expand my ideas to work out what's happening in a text
- I can develop ideas in detail about characters and events
- I can read between the lines in order to understand a text in different ways

Chapter 3

AF4 Identify and comment on the structure and organisation of texts

This chapter is going to show you how to

- Recognise the genre of a text and understand reader expectations

- Identify and comment on structural features in a review

- Understand the structure and presentation of a newspaper article

- Discuss the effect of presentational devices in multi-modal texts

- Understand why writers choose different forms for poems.

What's it all about?

You need to be able to recognise the different shapes and forms that texts take. This will help you quickly spot the devices that writers use.

1 Recognise the genre of a text and understand reader expectations

This lesson will
- help you to understand what genre means.

Genres are categories or types of texts or films – thriller, romance, action, adventure, fantasy, and so on. Texts within the same genre will share **similar features**.

Getting you thinking

1 Make a list of as many genres as you can and list some features you would expect to find in them.

> *Detective genre: a detective, a crime...*
>
> *Adventure genre: a quest, an obstacle/enemy...*

2 Look at these two **blurbs**. They are from the back covers of *Breathe* by Cliff McNish and *Can You Hear Me?* by Penny Kendal.

- What genre do you think they fall into?
- What kind of story would you expect if you decided to read either one of these books?

> Jack is used to danger. His asthma has nearly killed him more than once. But his new home has a danger he's never known before – the spirits of the dead.

> It sounded like a boy's voice, distant but clear. Leah jerked back, hitting her head on the wall for a second time that night. She knew she was awake this time.

Glossary

blurb: a short summary or taster of the story, which appears on the back cover of a book

CLIFF McNISH
Author of the DOOMSPELL trilogy

Are you brave enough?

Only the ghost knows the truth...

CAN YOU HEAR ME?

PENNY KENDAL

How does it work?

The books are both ghost or mystery stories. This is their genre. The fact that the titles sound mysterious and spooky might have helped you decide this. So might the mention of 'spirits of the dead' in the first blurb. Words and phrases such as 'never known', 'distant' and 'it sounded like' suggest that in each book there is a mystery to be unravelled.

Now you try it

Read this extract and decide what genre you think it falls into.

> They stayed at the edge of the Rusty Ruins.
>
> Occasionally hovercars would pass over the crumbling city, threading a slow search pattern across the sky. But the Smokies were old hands at hiding from satellites and aircrafts. They placed red herrings across the ruins – chemical glowsticks that gave off human-size pockets of heat – and covered the windows of their buildings with sheets of black Mylar. And of course the ruins were very large; finding seven people in what had once been a city of millions was no simple matter.

Top tips

Look for clues in the **nouns** in this piece. What are they telling you about the setting of this book?

Development activity

1 With a partner, identify which words helped you to decide on the genre. What do these words have in common?

2 Explain what other features you might expect, now that you know what genre this extract is from.

3 Now, write a short paragraph explaining what genre this extract comes from and how you decided this. Explain what this leads you to expect from the text.

Check your progress

LEVEL 4 I can recognise different types of text

LEVEL 5 I can recognise the genre of a text and understand reader expectations

LEVEL 6 I can discuss how writers create genre texts

This lesson will
- help you to explore how reviews are structured.

A good review of a book, play or film tends to be structured in a particular way so that the reader can clearly understand what the reviewer's opinion is and why.

Getting you thinking

Read this review of the film *Twilight*.

Twilight

(12A) 122mins

Based on the first of Stephenie Meyer's best-selling series of books, *Twilight* follows Bella Swan from sunny Phoenix to rainy Forks where she falls in love with the mysterious Edward Cullen.

At first, the pale Edward seems to be repulsed by Bella. But after he saves her from being crushed by a skidding van, he grows closer. It's the kind of on/off relationship most teens will understand. As Bella puts it: 'Your mood swings are giving me whiplash.'

Eventually, Bella works out that Edward is in fact undead and he admits that he's having real trouble not sucking her blood.

Kristen Stewart and Robert Pattinson, as the two leads, have chemistry and that is what makes this a successful adaptation.

Director Catherine Hardwicke has upped the action slightly, adding a couple of deaths. It remains tame stuff, though, not going anywhere near dark and failing to thrust any stakes from dusk til dawn.

Best line: Bella asks Edward: 'How long have you been 17?' He replies: 'A while.'

Best character: Edward is a great creation, a vampire whose fight against his true nature is constant.

RATING OUT OF FIVE: Two   *The Sun* (18 December 2008)

- For each paragraph, write one sentence summarising what it is about.
- What other features has the writer used to a) interest the reader and b) make his or her opinion of the film clear?

Now you try it

With a partner, read this review of the album *Down to Earth* by Jem.

Jem: Down to Earth

★★★☆☆

It didn't quite happen for Jemma Griffiths first time around. Her 2004 debut, *Finally Woken*, was expected to install her as the edgier Dido, with Dido-sized sales figures to match, but while the album sold half a million in the UK, her name was still greeted with: 'Jem who?'

The follow-up shows signs of a musical rethink. Produced by a quartet of big names, including Jeff Bass (who has worked with Eminem) and Greg Kurstin (Lily Allen), her slinky trip-hop now comes with Latin and Afrobeat accents.

The bad news: though it's utterly **sumptuous**, and occasionally sizzling, the album has lost the spook-pop quality that made the debut stand out. What a disappointment all round.

Glossary

sumptuous: splendid, extravagant

Pick out the parts of the review that

- remind the reader who Jem is
- give factual information about her new album
- provide three or four descriptive phrases about the music
- give the writer's opinion.

Development activity

Write a paragraph explaining how the review is structured and how this helps you to decide whether to buy the album or not.

Look closely at

- the title or headline
- the writer's use of paragraphs
- the language the writer uses
- any other features used.

Top tips

Thinking about the **purpose** of a text will help you to analyse its structure, whether it is a review or any other kind of text.

Remember

Quote from the text to support the points you make.

Check your progress

LEVEL 4	I can recognise when a text is organised and structured
LEVEL 5	I can identify structural features in an opinion text
LEVEL 6	I can discuss how writers develop their ideas in an opinion text

This lesson will
- help you to understand how newspaper articles are organised.

Understanding the presentational techniques and structural choices used in newspapers will help you understand the reports and articles that you read.

Getting you thinking

Read this article and try to identify how it is structured and presented.

1 — # Now school pupils are banned from eating tomato ketchup as part of healthy-eating drive
By Daily Mail Reporter — **2**

3 — *Ban: Tomato ketchup has been banned from the canteen in a string of Welsh primary schools and replaced with a sauce the cooks make*

4 — **Tomato ketchup has been banned from school canteens as part of a move towards healthier eating.**

Primary schools in the Vale of Glamorgan, South Wales, have removed the sauce because it contains 'too much salt and sugar'. The move has been branded 'daft' by some parents.

5 — Last week Marmite was banned from school breakfast clubs by Ceredigion Council, in Mid Wales, because of its salt content.

Sharon Chapman, 47, whose eight-year-old son Rory attends Peterston-Super-Ely Primary School said: 'He came home from school and said "We can't have ketchup any more".

'He can live without it and the healthy meals at the school are fantastic, but this seems one step too far.

'Tomato ketchup contains lycopene, which is good for you, but they say it's got a high level of salt and sugar.

'While it's not something you complain about, it seems a bit daft.' — **5**

Vale of Glamorgan Council leader Gordon Kemp said: 'It's all part of the healthy-eating programme and I think our council is one of the leading authorities in Wales in this respect.' — **6**

 — **7**

The Daily Mail (12 October 2008)

Can you name and explain the presentational devices 1–7?
Choose from the list below. The first few explanations have
been provided for you.

- Additional information – *this might link the event or topic to a wider context.*
- Lead paragraph – *this is sometimes called the 'nose'. It covers the basic information,* **who**, **what**, **where**, **why**, **when** *and* **how**.
- Headline –
- Explanation –
- Columns –
- By-line –
- Image –

Now you try it

1 Look at the article again and decide whether the six questions
(**who**, **what**, **where**, **why**, **when** and **how**) have been answered
in the lead paragraph.

2 What viewpoint do you think the report wants its
readers to have on the story? With a partner, discuss:
- how the report starts
- how many paragraphs present views **for** the decision to ban ketchup
- how many paragraphs present views **against** the decision
- how the report ends.

Development activity

Write a paragraph explaining why the report has been
organised and presented in this way.

You should explain how the structure
- helps to inform the reader
- encourages the reader to take a particular viewpoint.

Check your progress

LEVEL 4 I know that a newspaper article has a structure

LEVEL 5 I can understand the structure of a newspaper article

LEVEL 6 I can discuss how writers develop their ideas in a newspaper article

4 Discuss the effect of presentational devices in multi-modal texts

This lesson will
- help you to understand how websites are presented effectively.

Websites use presentational devices in various ways. You need to be able to identify those devices and also discuss the effect they have on readers.

Getting you thinking

Look carefully at this website.

navigation bar   video   images   downloads   search tool

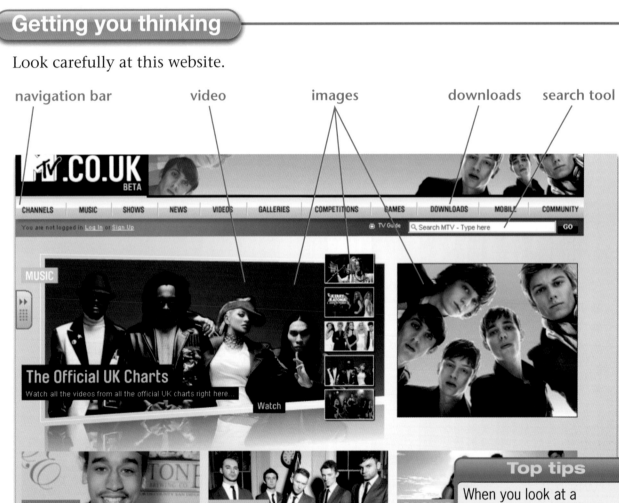

- Who do you think the website is aimed at?
- What is the purpose of the website?
- How do the presentational devices appeal to the readers of the website and support its purpose?
- Discuss your ideas with a partner.

Top tips

When you look at a website, you need to take into account not just what you can see but also what you can hear. That's because the text is multi-modal. It's not just a written text.

How does it work?

The website's purpose is to **inform** about the latest music news, releases and videos.

The target audience is **young people**. To appeal to teens, who like to be entertained, there is a lot happening on the page – it's packed full of interesting links and options.

The **layout** helps visitors access the information – the **navigation bar** at the top is written in black font on a grey background so this stands out and is easily seen. The **images** for Music and News help the viewer see at a glance what the top stories are. The **search tool** makes it even easier for viewers to choose where to go.

Now you try it

1 Look at all the options that visitors to this site have. Make a list of them.

2 Now look at the following features and discuss how these might appeal to the target audience:
- the choice of colours
- the kinds of images used
- the styles and sizes of font
- the positioning of headings on the page
- any other presentational devices you can spot

3 Write a paragraph explaining how the presentation should appeal to a teenage audience.

Development activity

Now look at another webpage of your own choice.
- Who do you think the website is aimed at?
- What is the purpose of the website?
- With a partner, prepare a presentation to the rest of the class. Explain how the presentational devices used on this website should appeal to its readers and support its purpose.

Check your progress

LEVEL 4 I can tell you about headings and images on websites

LEVEL 5 I can discuss the effect of presentational devices in multi-modal texts

LEVEL 6 I can analyse why writers present websites in certain ways

Understand why writers choose different forms for poems

This lesson will
● help you to understand different forms used in poetry.

Knowing about the form of a poem and understanding why poets choose different forms will help you to discuss and write about poems in more detail.

Getting you thinking

Read the following poem.

Valentine
My heart has made its mind up
And I'm afraid it's you.
Whatever you've got lined up,
My heart has made its mind up
And if you can't be signed up
This year, next year will do.
My heart has made its mind up
And I'm afraid it's you.

Wendy Cope

● What do you notice about the form of the poem?
● What do you think this form adds to the poem's meaning?

How does it work?

The poem is very structured. It uses a form called the 'Triolet'. The first line is repeated three times; the second line is also the last line, and there are repeated rhyming **refrains** such as 'lined up/mind up/signed up'.

The repeating structure of the poem might reflect the simplicity of Wendy Cope's message: regardless of what you feel, I love you, this isn't going to change.

The rhyming form also reminds us a little of the sort of verse you might see in a Valentine's card. There's even a short **metaphor** in there – 'if you can't be signed up…'.

Glossary

refrain: a repeated phrase, like the chorus of a song

Now you try it APP

Here is another poem about a girl's feelings for someone.

For the girl crying on the train

In a minute, you will brush the memory
Of his loveless kiss from your cheek;

In an hour, you will scour clean
His coffee cup smirk from the wood-grain;

In a day, you will slam shut the replay
Of the door's cold closing mouth
Upon your final encounter;

In a week or two, you will ride this train
Along a different track, talk about him
Like a character in a thin **novella**;

In a month, he will be a diverting ring-road
Around the city of your life.

In a year, wrapped in the shroud
Of someone else's arms,
You will bury him.

Mike Gould

> **Top tips**
>
> When looking at a poem you need to comment on what the form adds to the poem's meaning. This is really about the subtle feeling of the poem.

> **Glossary**
>
> **novella:** a very short novel

- What is the poem about? Discuss your ideas with a partner.

This poem is written in free verse – without rhyme and set rhythm – but you can still comment on how its form supports its meaning.

- How many stanzas are there? Are they all the same length or different lengths?
- Can you see any repeated lines or ideas? What do you think is their effect?
- What **similes** and **metaphors** does the writer use to describe how the girl feels about the boy who has left her?
- Look at the end of the poem: what is the effect of the short last line – and what does it mean?

> **Remember**
>
> A **simile** compares one thing to another using 'like' or 'as'.
>
> A **metaphor** says that something *is* something else.

Check your progress		
	LEVEL 4	I can tell you about the form of a poem
	LEVEL 5	I can understand why writers choose different forms for poems
	LEVEL 6	I can explain the effects of writers' choices in poetry

Level Booster

LEVEL 4

- I can recognise when a text is organised and structured
- I can recognise different types of text
- I can understand a sequence of events in a story and a beginning, middle and end
- I can tell you about how headings and bullet points can be used
- I can tell you about the form of a poem

LEVEL 5

- I can recognise the genre of a text and understand reader expectations
- I can identify structural features in an opinion text
- I can understand the structure of a newspaper article
- I can discuss the effect of presentational devices in multi-modal texts
- I can understand why writers choose different forms for poems

LEVEL 6

- I can identify how well a text is organised and structured
- I can discuss how writers develop their ideas in an opinion text
- I can analyse why writers present websites in certain ways
- I can explain the effects of writers' choices in poetry

AF5 Explain and comment on writers' use of language, including grammatical and literary features at word and sentence level

This chapter is going to show you how to

- Comment on metaphors
- Explore the tone and exact meaning of word choices
- Explore how and why authors vary sentence lengths
- Identify formal and informal register
- Comment on the effect of past and present tense narration.

What's it all about?

It is important to be able to discuss the way a text is **on the inside** (individual words and sentences), as well as its general meaning or purpose. What are the inner workings of the text? **How** has the author created the effects that you notice?

This lesson will
- help you to identify metaphors
- help you to explain how they make description come alive.

A metaphor is a kind of **image** – a **word picture**. It describes something as if it were something else.

Getting you thinking

Read this extract from a detective story.

Joe Bologna was just a little fish in a pond full of piranha. He cruised into town one November day when the sky was an upturned bowl of lead and the cold stabbed you in the guts. But he'd heard that the streets of Chicago were lined with dollar bills, and he hoped a plum job would land in his lap. He soon learned that life in the big city is not so much a bowl of cherries as a bunch of sour grapes. He wasn't the sharpest tool in the box, but he knew he was swimming against the tide, and he was looking for a way out of the water. When he met me, he thought I was throwing him a lifeline. Poor sucker – it was a baited hook, and he swallowed it.

With a partner, identify the metaphors in the opening sentences and discuss what you think they mean:

- 'Joe Bologna was just a little fish in a pond full of piranha.'
- 'He cruised into town one November day when the sky was an upturned bowl of lead and the cold stabbed you in the guts.'

Top tips

Metaphors are not quite the same as similes, which always contain 'like', 'as' or 'than'. Metaphors do compare two things, but in a less obvious way. Blink and you might miss them!

How does it work?

To understand metaphors, it helps to understand the word 'literally'. Joe Bologna is not **literally** a fish. In other words, he is not **really** a fish.

To comment on a metaphor, explain exactly how it fits what it describes. For example:

The author's metaphor says that Joe is like a 'little fish in a pond full of piranha'. This tells us that he is an ordinary, unimportant person surrounded by people far more dangerous than himself.

Now you try it

Explain what you think these metaphors mean. First, look back at the extract to read each one in context. Then explain why the metaphor fits what you think it is describing.

- 'not so much a bowl of cherries as a bunch of sour grapes'
- 'he wasn't the sharpest tool in the box'
- 'swimming against the tide'
- 'throwing him a lifeline'
- 'it was a baited hook, and he swallowed it'.

Development activity

Look at this poem. You might say the whole poem is an extended metaphor.

Snooker Player

He is a general.
He arranges ivory sounds.

He begins by breaking
The symmetry of delta.

He is a general.
He has enemies:
They are colours.

He aims to finish
With an empty field.

Shhh!
He is a general.
Words are a distraction.

The object of his game
Is complete silence.

Richard Freeman

Draw a table like the one below.

- In the left column, list the metaphors in this poem.
- In the right column, explain how the metaphor works.

For example, how is a snooker player like a general? You could illustrate both columns as you fill them in.

Metaphor	How does the metaphor work?

Check your progress

LEVEL 4 I can identify metaphors

LEVEL 5 I can explain what metaphors mean

LEVEL 6 I can explain how well metaphors fit what they describe

This lesson will
- help you to understand and explain how and why an author chooses words.

As a reader, you must try to understand why the author has chosen certain words – how they affect the precise meaning.

Getting you thinking

Read this description from the opening of Nella Larsen's 1920s novel, *Passing*.

> Chicago. August. A brilliant day, hot, with a brutal staring sun pouring down rays that were like molten rain. A day on which the very outlines of the buildings shuddered as if in protest at the heat. Quivering lines sprang up from baked pavements and wriggled along the shining car-tracks. The **automobiles** parked at the kerbs were a dancing blaze, and the glass of the shop-windows threw out a blinding radiance. Sharp particles of dust rose from the burning sidewalks, stinging the **seared** or dripping skins of wilting pedestrians. What small breeze there was seemed like the breath of a flame fanned by slow bellows.

- With a partner, pick out the most powerful examples of language that help you create an image in your mind.

Glossary

automobiles: cars

seared: burned or scorched

Now you try it

In 1818, the poet Percy Bysshe Shelley wrote a poem called 'Ozymandias'.

In the poem, the narrator meets a traveller who has just returned from Egypt. The traveller describes how he saw the ruined statue of an Egyptian pharaoh, Ozymandias in the desert.

The poem begins:

> I met a traveller from an antique land
> Who said: Two vast and **trunkless** legs of stone
> Stand in the desert.

Would the poem have the same impact if Shelley had begun it like this?

> I met some bloke who'd gone to this place abroad
> Who said: I saw this statue of two big legs
> made out of stone without the body
> Stuck in the ground.

- Discuss with a partner which opening you prefer.
- Which words in Shelley's opening create a more precise image in your head?

Development activity

Now imagine that this is Shelley's first draft of the rest of the poem. From the list below or your own imagination, pick stronger, more visual words that could replace those underlined.

> Near them on the sand,
> Half sunk, a <u>damaged</u> **visage** lies, whose frown
> And <u>puckered</u> lip and sneer of cold command
> Tell that its sculptor well those <u>feelings</u> read
> Which yet survive, stamped on these <u>dead</u> things

lifeless	breathless	shattered	broken
passions	emotions	wrinkled	curling

- Discuss how your replacements change the meaning or mood of the poem. How do they **feel** different?

Check your progress

LEVEL 4	I can see where an author could have used a different word
LEVEL 5	I can explain the effect that an author's word choice has
LEVEL 6	I can evaluate the author's choice of words

3 Comment on how and why authors vary sentence lengths

This lesson will
- help you to identify different types of sentence
- show you how to explain their effects.

Authors often vary their use of short, simple sentences with longer, more complex ones. You need to be able to **identify** the different types and **analyse their effect**.

Getting you thinking

Read this extract from the novel *Wolf Brother* by Michelle Paver. Here, Torak, a Stone-Age boy, is with his father who has been badly injured by a demon bear. They expect it to return.

> Torak spun round.
> The darkness was absolute. Everywhere he looked the shadows were bear-shaped.
> No wind.
> No birdsong.
> Just the crackle of the fire and the thud of his heart. The Forest itself was holding its breath.
> His father licked the sweat from his lips. 'It's not here yet,' he said. 'Soon. It will come for me soon … Quick. The knives.'
> Torak didn't want to swap knives. That would make it final. But his father was watching him with an intensity that allowed no refusal.

- With a partner, discuss how Michelle Paver uses different types and lengths of sentence to create tension.

Top tips

When looking at sentences, ask yourself what the author's **purpose** is in writing this part of the text. Is he or she trying to create tension? Is the purpose to shock or create an easy flow?

How does it work?

In the extract Michelle Paver uses **short** and **long** sentences. She also breaks grammatical rules by having some very short sentences with **no subject or verb**, as in 'No wind.' and 'No birdsong.'

Why? She wants us to feel the tension felt by Torak and his father as they wait for the bear. The forest is unnaturally still and quiet. The **short sentences** reflect this – as if someone is saying as little as possible to avoid attracting the bear.

Remember

A complete sentence must have a **verb** and a **subject** doing the verb. 'No wind.' is an incomplete sentence. The full sentence would be, 'There is no wind.'

Now you try it

Read the extract below. Torak is now in a graveyard, and is fleeing from clan chief Fin-Keddin.

> Mist floated in the hollows between the mounds, where the pale, ghostly skeletons of hemlock reared above his head, and the purple stalks of dying willowherb released their eerily drifting down. All around stood the dark, listening trees: trees that stayed green all winter, that never slept. In the branches of the tallest yew perched three ravens, watching him. He wondered which one was the clan guardian.
>
> A baying of dogs behind him.
>
> He was caught in a trap. Clever Fin-Keddin: throwing his net wide, then tightening it around the quarry.

1 In groups of seven, read the passage aloud, taking one sentence each. Speak your sentence to reflect its mood, as suggested by its length. Be dramatic!

2 Discuss these questions:
   - What types of sentence are used in the first paragraph? How do they help create an eerie mood?
   - What is unusual about the fifth sentence, 'A baying of dogs behind him.'? What is the effect of this sentence?
   - What do you notice about the final two sentences? What is their effect?

Development activity APP

Write a paragraph or two describing the atmosphere Michelle Paver creates in this passage. Remember to think about the length of sentences she uses, and to give examples from the text.

Check your progress	LEVEL 4	I can identify different types of sentence
	LEVEL 5	I can explain how different sentences are constructed
	LEVEL 6	I can comment on how authors use a variety of sentences for effect

This lesson will
- help you to understand and explain how authors use formal and informal language in dialogue.

The register (or tone) of text or dialogue can be formal or informal. In fiction, characters may vary the register in which they speak.

Getting you thinking

In the extract below, two friends speak to each other, then to a head teacher. Notice the different styles of speech.

> Wallace grinned as a red-headed boy slouched into view. 'Hey – Ginger! What you doin' 'ere, then?'
>
> The boy leaned against the wall. 'All right, Jonah? Me? I dunno. I was mindin' me own business and Miss says to me what was she on about and, like, totally loses it and says I got to report to Mr Rogers.'
>
> 'That's harsh, man!'
>
> 'Yeah – well out of order. What about you?'
>
> 'Well, you know Jane Smith, right? Well –'
>
> The oak door before them opened abruptly to reveal a bald man in a dark suit. Both boys straightened up. The head waved them in.
>
> 'The usual suspects, I see. Jones, I believe I informed you on Monday that if any member of staff saw fit to send you here before the end of term I would be contacting your parents. What is it this time?'
>
> 'Sir, Mr Amos said my concern for animal welfare was inappropriate.'
>
> 'I see. On what grounds?'
>
> 'Er – In the lab, sir.'
>
> 'I mean why, Jones!'
>
> 'I don't really know sir. I think it was because I let the rats out, sir, and one ate Jane Smith's sandwiches.'
>
> 'And how do you justify this behaviour?'
>
> 'I think it was hungry, sir!'

How does it work?

Wallace and Ginger speak in an **informal register**. They use slang phrases such as 'well out of order' and casual pronunciation, as in 'dunno', 'Yeah' and 'mindin''. The head speaks **formally** – 'informed you' (told you); 'if any member of staff saw fit' (if any teacher decided) – to assert his authority.

Now you try it

- Discuss with a partner what other informal phrases and pronunciation the boys use.
- How does Wallace speak to the head? How does his speech change?

Development activity

Compare the language used in the letter and the postcard below. Comment on the choice of words and the kinds of sentence used.

Letter 1

> Dear Sir,
>
> I wish to apply for the position of pool attendant at Shirehall Leisure Centre.
>
> I am a fit and responsible recent school leaver, with a great deal of experience in a wide range of sports. I have completed my Gold Life Saving Qualification, and have a certificate in Advanced Health and Safety. I would appreciate the opportunity to fulfil a useful role, and one which could lead to a career in the leisure industry.
>
> I enclose two references and look forward to hearing from you.
>
> Yours faithfully,
> James Lodge

Letter 2

> Yo Kiddo!
> This is coming at you all the way from Tenerife, where I'm having a wicked time. All day on the beach, all night in the clubs! No shark attacks yet – which is cool. But if I see anyone thrashing about I'll dive in and be a hero. Good practice for the new job.
> See you (maybe...) in a week, Jimbo

Check your progress

LEVEL 4	I can find examples of formal and informal language
LEVEL 5	I can explain why writers use formal and informal language
LEVEL 6	I can comment on the effect of formal and informal language

Comment on the effect of past and present tense narration

This lesson will
- help you to identify the tense used in a narrative
- help you to comment on how effectively the author uses it.

Verbs come in **different tenses**: the past, present and future. Stories can be told in the past tense ('I was') or present tense ('I am'). Predictions are in the future tense – we rarely see the future tense ('I will') in storytelling.

Top tips

The **past continuous** tense is sometimes used in a novel, but not for the whole novel. Here are some examples: 'When I was young, we **used to spend** the whole winter outside sledging.' 'I **was going** to visit my friend'.

Getting you thinking

With a partner, read these two extracts from *Of Mice and Men*, and discuss why the writer has chosen each tense.

Present tense

> There is a path through the willows and among the **sycamores**, a path beaten hard by boys coming down from the ranches to swim in the deep pool, and beaten hard by tramps who come wearily down from the highway in the evening to jungle-up near water. In front of the low horizontal limb of a giant sycamore, there is an ash pile made by many fires.

Past tense

> The first man stopped short in the clearing, and the follower nearly ran over him. He took off his hat and wiped the sweat-band with his forefinger and snapped the moisture off. His huge companion dropped his blankets and flung himself down and drank from the surface of the green pool; drank with long gulps, snorting into the water like a horse.

Glossary

sycamore: a type of tree common in Britain and North America

How does it work?

John Steinbeck uses the **present tense** to set the scene. This creates a sense of timelessness, as if the place described has always been like this, and will always be visited by boys and tramps.

Steinbeck then moves into the **past tense** to describe what happened there.

Now you try it

In this extract from the novel *Dracula* by Bram Stoker, Jonathan Harker is keeping a diary of his stay in Count Dracula's castle.

> When I went into the dining room, breakfast was prepared; but I could not find the Count anywhere. So I breakfasted alone. It is strange that as yet I have not seen the Count eat or drink. He must be a very peculiar man!

1 Which **two** tenses are used in this extract?

2 What is the effect of using the second tense – how does it make the story more immediate?

Development activity

In this later extract, Harker is at his window, and hears a woman begging Dracula to return her child to her.

> Somewhere high overhead, probably on the tower, I heard the voice of the Count calling in his harsh, metallic whisper. His call seemed to be answered from far and wide by the howling of wolves. Before many minutes had passed a pack of them poured, like a pent-up dam when liberated, through the wide entrance into the courtyard.
>
> There was no cry from the woman, and the howling of the wolves was but short. Before long they streamed away singly, licking their lips.
>
> I could not pity her, for I knew now what had become of her child, and she was better dead.
>
> What shall I do? What can I do? How can I escape from this dreadful **thrall** of night and gloom and fear?

How do the different tenses help to

○ describe the incident with the wolves
○ reveal Harker's feelings and concerns
○ make us curious about what might happen next?

Glossary

thrall: spell or hold

Check your progress

LEVEL 4	I can understand the three main tenses (past, present, future)
LEVEL 5	I can comment on an author's choice of tense
LEVEL 6	I can identify different tenses and comment in detail on their effect

Level Booster

LEVEL 4

- I know what a metaphor is
- I can see where an author could have used a different word
- I can identify different types of sentence
- I can give examples of formal and informal language
- I can identify the three main tenses

LEVEL 5

- I can explain what metaphors mean
- I can explain the effect of an author's word choice
- I can explain how different types of sentence are formed
- I can explain when characters use formal and informal language
- I can comment on an author's choice of tense

LEVEL 6

- I can comment on how well metaphors fit what they describe
- I can comment on how choice of words affects tone
- I can comment on how authors use a variety of sentences for effect
- I can comment on the features of formal and informal dialogue
- I can identify variations on the three basic tenses and comment on their use

Chapter 5

AF6 Identify and comment on writers' purposes and viewpoints, and the overall effect of the text on the reader

This chapter is going to show you how to

- Identify the writer's purpose in creating the text
- Identify the viewpoint of a text
- Identify the effect the text has on the reader
- Explain your ideas.

What's it all about?

It's important to be able to understand why the writer is writing and what his or her point of view is. Then you will be able to understand how well the message comes across to the reader.

1 Identify the writer's purpose in creating a text

This lesson will

● help you to respond to the writer's purpose in producing a text.

Every text is created for a reason. Often an author will have a number of purposes in mind when they write and you need to bear this in mind when you are analysing a text.

Getting you thinking

Romeo and Juliet is a famous play by William Shakespeare. You might know something about the characters or storyline already. It has been interpreted in many different ways in films, cartoons, ballets, books and other media.

Look at this page from the opening of a modern graphic novel version of *Romeo and Juliet*. It is by Sonia Leong and is set in Tokyo. Yakuza are traditional organised crime gangs in Japan.

● Discuss with a partner why you think Sonia Leong has chosen to tell the story of Romeo and Juliet in this way.

Present-day Tokyo. Two teenagers, Romeo and Juliet, fall in love. But their rival Yakuza families are at war.

Now you try it

1 What do you think writers try to do in the opening section of a book? Discuss with a partner.

2 Look back at the graphic novel page. What does it tell you about the characters and the setting?

- Look at the two main characters in the centre. How do they feel about each other? Explain your ideas to your partner, giving evidence for your ideas.
- With your partner, point to the parts of the text that tell you about the place where the story is set.

3 Now write a paragraph explaining

- one of the **purposes** of the extract
- how you know this (your **evidence**)
- how your evidence proves your **point**.

Remember

Your evidence here will be your description of details from the image – you are 'quoting' what you see, not what you read.

Development activity APP

Now look at the **prologue** of Shakespeare's *Romeo and Juliet*.

Shakespeare set the play in Verona, a city in Italy.

background information on the families' feud

Two households, both alike in dignity,
In fair Verona, where we lay our scene,
From ancient grudge break to new mutiny,
Where civil blood makes civil hands unclean.
From forth the fatal loins of these two foes
A pair of star-cross'd lovers take their life;

they are equally important and powerful

hints that this is a tragic love story

1 Does Sonia Leong give the same information in her extract as Shakespeare does in his **prologue**? Discuss with your partner how she shows that

- there are two families
- the families are both powerful
- there is a feud
- this is a tragic love story.

Glossary

prologue: an introduction to a story or play; it introduces themes and ideas

2 Which do you think is the more effective text for someone your age? Explain your point of view.

Check your progress

LEVEL 4	I can identify the main purpose of a text
LEVEL 5	I can clearly identify the main purpose of a text and start to explain how I know this
LEVEL 6	I can give precise evidence for my ideas about the purpose of a text

This lesson will
- help you to identify the way a writer establishes the viewpoint of a text

You need to be able to identify the **viewpoint** of a text. This means asking yourself from whose position or perspective the text is written. You also need to use your skills in identifying the purpose and audience of the text.

Getting you thinking

1 Look at the front of this leaflet published by Parentline.
- First, decide who the target audience is. The clue is in the title!
- What do you think the purpose of the leaflet is?

2 Now look at the picture. With a partner, discuss what you think it tells us about the viewpoint of the leaflet. Is the image more likely to appeal to teenagers or parents?

3 Copy and complete this table to show what the image suggests about the leaflet's viewpoint.

'wot u up 2 l8r? lol!'	This suggests that teenagers use language that parents find difficult to understand and that this might cause problems between them.
The girl is putting on lipstick	
The girl has her iPod headphones on while her mother is talking to her	
The girl is talking on her mobile phone	

How does it work?

The image presents the point of view that teenagers are difficult to understand or get on with. The way the girl is shown ignoring her mother suggests that she is in the wrong, so this gives you the idea that the leaflet will present the viewpoint of parents rather than teenagers.

Now you try it

However, to work out whether this interpretation is correct, you now need to look more closely at the written text. Look at the large caption.

first person – mother's voice ————

shows she doesn't feel she's getting ———— through to her daughter

I try to tell her enough's enough.

This sentence supports the idea that this leaflet is written from the parents' viewpoint.

Now read the rest of the written text from the leaflet:

With a partner, discuss how the voice in this extract is different from the sentence above it.

It's easy to think your teenager doesn't want anything more to do with you. When they seem to ignore all you say or do, it's difficult to see that being a teenager can be very tough.

- How has the voice changed?
- Who do you think is 'saying' this line?
- How has the viewpoint changed?

Development activity

Now write a paragraph starting with:

I think that the viewpoint presented in the leaflet will be...

Think about

- who the leaflet is aimed at
- what its purpose is
- what different points of view it presents.

Remember

Give evidence for your points and explain why you chose each example.

Check your progress

LEVEL 4 I can make comments about the viewpoint the writer is using

LEVEL 5 I can clearly identify the viewpoint in a text and start to explain how I know this

LEVEL 6 I can explain the viewpoint used in a text clearly with close reference to the text

This lesson will
● help you to explain the effect a text has on the reader.

A writer chooses a viewpoint and language very carefully
to have a particular effect on you as the reader.

Getting you thinking

1 Dracula is a well-known character. With a
partner, make a list of things you already
know about Dracula.

2 Read this extract from the novel *Dracula*
by Bram Stoker, written in 1897. The
narrator, Jonathan Harker, is describing
his journey to Dracula's castle.

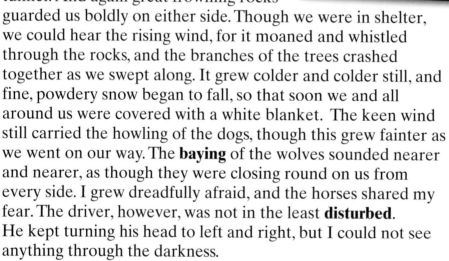

Soon we were **hemmed in** with trees,
which in places arched right over the
roadway till we passed as through a
tunnel. And again great frowning rocks
guarded us boldly on either side. Though we were in shelter,
we could hear the rising wind, for it moaned and whistled
through the rocks, and the branches of the trees crashed
together as we swept along. It grew colder and colder still, and
fine, powdery snow began to fall, so that soon we and all
around us were covered with a white blanket. The keen wind
still carried the howling of the dogs, though this grew fainter as
we went on our way. The **baying** of the wolves sounded nearer
and nearer, as though they were closing round on us from
every side. I grew dreadfully afraid, and the horses shared my
fear. The driver, however, was not in the least **disturbed**.
He kept turning his head to left and right, but I could not see
anything through the darkness.

● Discuss with a partner how you think Stoker wants you to feel.
● Pick out three examples of powerful language from the
extract and explain to your partner how each example
makes you feel.
● Why do you think Bram Stoker chose to tell the story
from Jonathan Harker's viewpoint, using a first-person
'I' narrator?

Glossary

hemmed in: surrounded
baying: howling
disturbed: upset

How does it work?

The author is attempting to create a tense and frightening atmosphere.

The extract is written in the **first person** (using 'I' instead of 'he') and this makes us feel as if we are sharing this creepy journey with the narrator.

Stoker uses language that **appeals to the senses**, describing what the narrator can see ('great frowning rocks'), hear ('the baying of the wolves') and feel ('it grew colder and colder still').

The **vivid vocabulary** suggests the narrator's fear, which the reader is encouraged to share.

Remember

Ask yourself: Who is speaking? Why this choice of words?

Now you try it

1 Note down the words and short phrases that Stoker uses to create a tense atmosphere.

2 Using your notes, complete this table.

Description	What this means	How it makes you feel
'It grew colder and colder still'	The repetition of the word 'colder' shows that the atmosphere is becoming increasingly hostile and unfriendly.	It makes me understand the journey from the narrator's viewpoint. He is becoming more uneasy.

Development activity

Now write a paragraph that answers this question:

● How does Bram Stoker make the reader feel in this extract?
   You can use this structure to help you:

   Bram Stoker wanted to make the reader feel...
   He does this by...
   This makes the reader feel...

Check your progress

LEVEL 4 : I can make comments about the effect a text has on the reader

LEVEL 5 : I can start to explain my ideas about the effect of a text on the reader

LEVEL 6 : I can explain how the effect on the reader has been created

This lesson will
- help you to explain how writers make choices to create an effect on the reader.

These pages will help you to explain why a writer chooses specific language to create an effect on the reader.

Getting you thinking

> He was alone, and in the dark; and when he reached out for the matches, the matches were put into his hand.
>
> *Kevin Crossley-Holland*

This is a very short, short story. However, it has everything we need to understand what is happening and to have an effect on us as readers.

- Explain to your partner what you think happens in the story.

Now you try it

Read this extract from *Dracula*. The narrator, Jonathan Harker, has just arrived at the castle of Count Dracula in the remote region of Transylvania. He has been sent on business from England.

Glossary

calèche: a type of horse-drawn carriage

traps: bags

projecting: sticking out

I must have been asleep, for certainly if I had been fully awake I must have noticed the approach of such a remarkable place. In the gloom the courtyard looked of considerable size, and as several dark ways led from it under great round arches, it perhaps seemed bigger than it really is.

When the **calèche** stopped, the driver jumped down and held out his hand to assist me to alight. His hand actually seemed like a steel vice that could have crushed mine if he had chosen. Then he took my **traps**, and placed them on the ground beside me as I stood close to a great door, old and studded with large iron nails, and set in a **projecting** doorway of massive stone. I could see even in the dim light that the stone was massively carved, but that the carving had been much worn by time and weather.

I stood in silence where I was, for I did not know what to do. Of bell or knocker there was no sign; through these frowning walls and dark window openings it was not likely that my voice could penetrate.

- With a partner, choose one sentence or phrase from each paragraph which describes the door, doorway or castle .
- Choose the sentences or phrases which have the most effect on you as a reader. Copy each one on to a different sticky note.

Development activity

Stick the notes into your book in the order they appear in the extract. Under each note write a paragraph explaining

- the effect of these words on the reader
- why Bram Stoker chose to use them.

For example:

> 'several dark ways led from it under great round arches'

The effect of this phrase on the reader is to emphasise that the castle is huge by using the word 'great'. It also makes the castle seem mysterious as it says that the passages were 'dark', which makes them sound frightening. I think that Bram Stoker used these words to make the reader understand that the narrator is in an intimidating place.

Check your progress

LEVEL 4 I can make comments on the effect a text has on the reader

LEVEL 5 I can give some explanation for the way a writer has created an effect on the reader

LEVEL 6 I can explain how the effect on the reader has been created

Level Booster

LEVEL 4

- I can identify the main purpose of a text
- I can comment on the writer's viewpoint
- I can comment on the way the writer makes the reader feel
- I can give some evidence for my ideas

LEVEL 5

- I can identify what the writer is trying to achieve (the writer's purpose)
- I can identify the writer's viewpoint
- I can identify the effect a text has on the reader
- I can explain my ideas

LEVEL 6

- I can clearly explain the purpose of a text
- I can clearly explain the viewpoint of the writer in more complex texts
- I can clearly identify the effect on the reader and say how that effect has been created
- I can give detailed evidence for my opinions at word level
- I can give detailed evidence for my opinions at sentence level
- I can give detailed evidence for my opinions at whole text level

Chapter 6

AF7 Relate texts to their social, cultural and historical traditions

This chapter is going to show you how to

- Explore conventions in texts

- Understand how historical context affects the conventions, content and form of a text

- Explain how context affects the way we read

- Explain how changing contexts affect the way texts are read.

What's it all about?

Understanding why, when, where and how a text was written helps us have a better appreciation of the text as a whole.

This lesson will
- help you to recognise and write about conventions in texts.

Conventions are the typical features readers expect to see in particular texts. These could be

- **language conventions** (for example, we expect fairy stories to begin with the words 'Once upon a time')
- **conventions to do with ideas or structure** (for example, we expect most fairy tales to end happily)
- **conventions to do with appearance or presentation** (we expect young children's books to have bigger writing and lots of pictures).

When you can identify such conventions you are reading at Level 5.

Getting you thinking

One newspaper convention is that

- on the **front page** you expect to find stories about news or politics
- on the **back page** you usually find sports stories.

This is a convention to do with **ideas and structure**.

Now look at this newspaper headline.

Race plan went out of window

With a partner, discuss what you think the article would be about if it was

- on the front page of a newspaper
- on the back page of a newspaper.

Now you try it

Now read the beginning of the article:

Olympics: Race plan went out of window, says Ohuruogu

Sprinter is first UK 400m champion since Liddell Londoner may not run on home soil in 2012 games

Christine Ohuruogu, who last night won Britain's first Olympic 400m gold medal since Eric Liddell in 1924, admitted that she had run the race blind. 'I had a race plan but as usual it went out the window,' she said. 'I was in my own world. People said "Did you know Sanya [Richards] had gone off very hard?" but she was in lane seven and I couldn't see her.'

The Guardian (20 August 2008)

Now let's think about the conventions concerning the **appearance** or **presentation** of the article.

- What do you notice about the font size of the **headline**, the **sub-headings** and the **first paragraph**?
- Why do you think these different font sizes are used?

Development activity

Finally, what about conventions to do with **language**?

This article uses a typical phrase a sportsperson or sportswriter might use. Christine's race plan 'went *out the window*'. This is a **metaphor**, as Christine didn't literally throw her plan out of a window! It means she suddenly abandoned the way she had planned to run the race.

Here are two other typical phrases we might expect in such a report:

- Christine… admitted she had **run the race blind**
- 'I was **in my own world**'

Discuss with a partner what each phrase means in the context of the race.

Remember

Conventions are the *typical* features we expect to see in a text. They can be to do with

- **language** (the words used)
- **ideas/structure** (the things that are written about and the order they are in)
- **appearance/ presentation** (how they are presented).

Glossary

metaphor: a comparison made between one thing and another

This lesson will
- help you to think about the context and conventions of a ballad.

When a text is written can affect the form chosen and the type of conventions used.

Getting you thinking

1 Which of these forms of writing would you be most likely to use today to reply to a party invitation?
- a letter
- a telegram
- an e-mail
- a text message

2 Which do you think would have been used 200 years ago?

Some texts we use today existed then as well: for example, newspapers, novels (although these were often published in magazine form), letters and poems. Some, however, are less popular today but at the time were important ways to express emotions and spread news.

One such type was the **ballad**, a story usually told in rhyming verses. Ballads were easy to remember, and often started as songs which were passed from one person to another.

Often, there is a real-life story behind the ballad. Read this example, written in about 1805.

The Female Transport

Come all young girls, both far and near and listen unto me
While unto you I do unfold what proved my destiny
My mother died when I was young, it caused me to deplore
And I did get my way too soon upon my native shore

Sarah Collins is my name most dreadful is my fate
My father reared me tenderly the truth I do relate
Till enticed by bad company along with many more
It led to my discovery upon my native shore

My trial it approached fast before the judge I stood
And when the judge's sentence passed it fairly chilled my blood
Crying you must be transported for fourteen years or more
And go from hence across the seas unto **Van Diemen's shore**

It hurt my heart when on a coach I my native town passed by
To see so many I did know it made me heave a sigh
Then to a ship was sent with speed along with many more
Whose aching hearts did grieve to go unto Van Diemen's shore

The sea was rough ran mountains high with us poor girls 'twas hard
No one but God to us came nigh no one did us regard
At length alas we reached the land it grieved us ten times more
That wretched place Van Diemen's Land far from our native shore

They chained us two by two and whipped and lashed along
They cut off our **provisions** if we did the least thing wrong
They march us in the burning sun until our feet are sore
So hard's our lot now we are got to Van Diemen's shore

[…]

Come all young men and **maidens** do bad company forsake
If tongue can tell our overthrow it will make your heart to ache
Young girls I pray be ruled by me your wicked ways give o'er
For fear like us you spend your days upon Van Diemen's shore

Glossary

Van Diemen's shore: Van Dieman's land was an early name for Tasmania, near Australia.

provisions: food and water

maidens: young girls

Now you try it

Without knowing much about the historical background to this ballad, discuss with a partner:

- What story is being told?
- What happened to Sarah Collins?

You can immediately see certain conventions about the *form* of the ballad: for example, it has **verses** of **four lines** each.

- On your own, note down **two other features** which you notice about the ballad.

This is a poem written over 200 years ago.

- What clues are there in the **language** – the choice of words – to tell us this? (For example, do we still say 'morn' for 'morning'?)

Top tips

Think about repeated lines and the sound or rhyme patterns.

Development activity

Now let's find out about the real historical background to this poem.

1 First, read these facts about the transportation of convicts to Australia.

- The transport of convicts to Australia began in the late 18th century as British prisons became overcrowded.
- Crime in British cities had increased during the Industrial Revolution.
- The first ships carrying British convicts arrived in Botany Bay in January 1788.
- Transportation peaked in 1833 when 36 ships took nearly 7000 people to Australia.

2 Then, read this extract from a local newspaper, the
Sydney Cove Chronicle, in 30 June 1790. It reports the
arrival of four 'transports' – convict ships – in Australia.

The landing of those who remained alive despite their misuse upon
the recent voyage, could not fail to horrify those who watched. As
they came on shore, these **wretched** people were hardly able to
move hand or foot. Such as could not carry themselves upon their
legs, crawled upon all fours. Those who, through their **afflictions**,
were not able to move, were thrown over the side of the ships, as
sacks of flour would be thrown, into the small boats.

Some expired in the boats; others as they reached the shore. Some
fainted and were carried by those who fared better. More had not
the opportunity even to leave their ocean prisons for as they came
upon decks, the fresh air only hastened their **demise**.

A sight most outrageous to our eyes were the marks of leg irons upon
the convicts, some so deep that one could **nigh on** see the bones.

3 Discuss with a partner:
  - Having read about the facts behind the 'transport' of
    convicts, why do you think Sarah Collins chose to
    tell her tale?
  - Why do you think it survives in ballad form?
  - How do you think audiences in her own time would
    have reacted to the ballad?
  - Do we react differently reading it today?

Glossary

wretched: poor, in an unhappy state

afflictions: injuries or suffering

expired: died

demise: death

nigh on: almost

4 Finally, write a short account of 'The Female Transport'.
In it you should explain how the poem reflects its time.

Start…

*First of all, 'The Female Transport' is in the form of
a ballad. It is written in…*

The language sounds quite… but…

The subject of the ballad is…

It tells the story of…

The audience at the time would probably have been…

Sarah Collins' purpose is to…

Check your progress

LEVEL 4 I can identify time context in a newspaper and a ballad

LEVEL 5 I can read the time context in a newspaper and a ballad

LEVEL 6 I can explain in detail the time context in a newspaper and a ballad

This lesson will
- help you to read the context of a war poster.

Good readers can explain how the **context** of a text can affect its meaning. The context means the **time, place and social setting** in which a text was written.

When we read a text, we need to look a little bit deeper at the context – when, why and how a text was produced – and consider how we view it in the present day.

Getting you thinking

Look at this famous poster produced in 1914.

With a partner, discuss the following questions about the text and its context.

Context

- Given that this poster was produced in 1914, what do you think its purpose was?
- Who do you think it was aimed at?
- Where do you think it would have been displayed?

Text

- Describe how the poster looks – what sort of language does it use?
- How does the poster combine words and images to achieve its effect?
- Would the poster persuade you to join the army, if you saw it on a wall now? Why or why not?

Now you try it

Most Army recruitment advertisements are now shown on television, or online. We are in a **different context** today – people know much more about war and its effects.

1 On your own, write down three positive things you can think of about joining the Army. Now write down three negative things

2 Join with a partner and compare what you wrote.

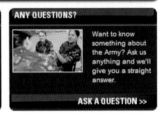

3 Now look at the top half of the army website. Does it match with any of your positive reasons for joining the Army?

4 With a partner, discuss what seems to be the **main** way the Army is selling itself to people visiting the website.

Development activity

Prepare a short presentation in which you compare the different ways the Army advertises itself in

- the Kitchener poster
- the website.

Make sure you talk about

- the context – for example, when the Kitchener poster was produced and why.
- the words and images – how they are presented, what they suggest and what effects they have.

Check your progress

LEVEL 4   I can spot the context of army recruitment texts

LEVEL 5   I can read army recrutiment posters in context

LEVEL 6   I can explain how the context of army recruitment posters affects how we read them

This lesson will
- help you to develop your understanding of how changing contexts affect our reading.

This means that the same **texts seem to change** when read in different contexts. It is not that the texts change, of course, but that **we read them differently**. What was written for one place, time or social setting looks different in another.

Getting you thinking

Look at this 1930s advertisement for smoking. It comes from a different time with different attitudes. By today's advertising standards, it would be illegal!

- How does it encourage smoking? Is it aimed at anyone in particular?

How does it work?

The image, brand name and caption all combine to make smoking – and these cigarettes in particular – look attractive.

- The 'cool', stylish woman set against a restful purple background links smoking with style and sophistication.

- The word 'Westminster' is in the lively colours of a flame. Westminster is the area of London world famous for political power, even more so in the 1930s. So the name links the brand with power and prestige.

- The choice of words, 'Women also prefer them', adds class and encourages female buyers.

It is very different today. Women smoking are often shown negatively in the media. We might, therefore, read the advert differently.

Now you try it

Look at this advertisement from our own time, which also combines words, colours and captions in a striking way.

In groups, decide how this combination is put together to make smoking seem unattractive.

- Is it aimed at any audience in particular?
- What worries does it try to increase? How?

Top tips

When 'reading' an image, keep asking yourself: why?

Why this background choice? Why this model? Why have the text in this position/font/colour/size?

Development activity APP

Alf Tupper was a character in the *Rover* comic of the 1950s. He welded all day, smoked, drank and ate unhealthily, but still usually beat the 'professionals' on the sports field.

Read this extract from the comic and answer the questions below.

> Alf sniffed. His overalls had holes in them. He needed a haircut. The state of his fingernails would have caused a **manicurist** to swoon. Yet he had a great reputation as an athlete. Alf was crazy about running and jumping, and about little else – except, perhaps, eating. He was always hungry.
>
> 'What chances have you got against the stars this afternoon?' asked Sam Kessick, the owner of the café. Alf grinned. 'I can run 'em,' he replied. 'Well, let's have a stoke-up.'
>
> 'Fried fish and chips?' asked Kessick. 'If you had turkey and plum pudding, I'd still have fish an' chips,' said Alf.

Glossary

manicurist: someone who treats hands and fingernails (as their profession)

- What does the extract suggest about the attitude towards sportsmen in the 1950s?
- What would we think about a sportsman like Alf nowadays?
- How have our ideas on health and fitness changed?

Discuss your ideas with a partner and then prepare a short presentation to explain these to the rest of the class.

Check your progress

LEVEL 4	I can spot a different health context in a 1950s text
LEVEL 5	I can explain the different health contexts of a 1950s text
LEVEL 6	I can discuss in detail how health contexts affect our reading of a 1950s text

Level Booster

LEVEL 4

- Identify different time, place and social settings in the texts you read
- Identify character and setting in texts
- Comment on character and setting in texts about different societies
- Compare texts in the same genre

LEVEL 5

- Compare and contrast conventions in texts
- Identify texts in context (time, place and social setting)
- Make some explanation of how contexts (time, place and social settings) affect how texts are read
- Explain the extent to which context affects how texts are written

LEVEL 6

- Recognise conventions in a literary text
- Recognise conventions in a non-literary text
- Discuss in some detail how the same literary form is used differently in different periods
- Discuss in some detail how the meaning of the same text can change over time
- Discuss in some detail how ideas in texts are treated differently in different times and places

Chapter 7

Longer texts and reading activities

What's it all about?

Bringing all the Assessment Focuses together.

The sun hovered briefly on the horizon, then dipped below. At once, the clouds rolled in – first red, then mauve, silver, green and black as if all the colours in the world were being sucked into a vast melting pot. A single **frigate bird** soared over the **mangroves**, its own colours lost in the chaos behind it. The air was close. Rain hung waiting. There was going to be a storm.

The single engine Cessna Skyhawk SP circled twice before coming in to land. It was the sort of plane that would barely have been noticed, flying in this part of the world. That was why it had been chosen. If anyone had been curious enough to check the registration number printed under the wing, they would have learned that this plane belonged to a photographic company based in Jamaica. This was not true. There was no company and it was already too dark to take photographs.

There were three men in the aircraft. They were all dark skinned, wearing faded jeans and loose open-neck shirts. The pilot had long black hair, deep brown eyes and a thin scar running down the side of his face. He had met his two passengers only that afternoon. They had introduced themselves as Carlo and Marc but he doubted these were their real names. He knew that their journey had begun a long time ago, somewhere in Eastern Europe. He knew that this short flight was the last leg. He knew what they were carrying. Already, he knew too much.

The pilot glanced down at the multifunction display in the control panel. The illuminated computer screen was warning him of the storm that was closing in. That didn't worry him. Low clouds and rain gave him cover. The authorities were less **vigilant** during a storm. Even so, he was nervous. He had flown into Cuba many times, but never here. And tonight he would have preferred to have been going almost anywhere else.

Cayo Esqueleto. Skeleton Key.

There it was, stretching out before him, thirty-eight kilometres long and nine kilometres across at its widest point. The sea around it, which had been an extraordinary, brilliant blue until a few minutes ago, had suddenly darkened, as if someone had thrown a switch. Over to the west, he could make out the twinkling lights of Puerto Madre, the island's second biggest town. The main airport was further north, outside the capital of Santiago. But that wasn't where he was heading. He pressed on the joystick and the plane veered to the right, circling over the forests and mangrove swamps that surrounded the old, abandoned airport at the bottom end of the island.

AF 2   What information are we told about each of the three men in paragraph 3?

AF 3   In this extract, the pilot is going through a challenging experience. What deductions can you make about how the pilot is feeling? Make sure you refer to the text in your answer.

AF 4   What new information do we learn in each paragraph? What stage of the journey is reached in each new paragraph?

AF 5   There are lots of short sentences in this passage. Why do you think the writer uses them? What is the effect on the reader?

AF 6   Horowitz is telling the story from the pilot's viewpoint in this extract. How does he make the reader feel about the pilot? Try to find examples from the text to explain your ideas.

AF 7   How does Anthony Horowitz build up an unfamiliar world for his novel to take place in? You should think about
   - the names of places, people and machines
   - how the characters look and behave
   - the geographical setting and climate.

Add a comment on how each of these could suggest danger.

Glossary

frigate bird: a tropical bird with a long bill, wide wingspan and a forked tail

mangroves: tropical evergreen trees that grow along the coast

vigilant: watchful or strict

Cayo Esqueleto: 'Skeleton Key' in Spanish

I decided to clean out the fridge the other day. We don't usually clean out our fridge – we just box it up every four or five years and send it off to the Centers for Disease Control in Atlanta with a note to help themselves to anything that looks scientifically promising – but we hadn't seen one of the cats for a few days and I had a vague recollection of having glimpsed something furry on the bottom shelf towards the back. (Turned out to be a large piece of **Gorgonzola**.)

So there I was, down on my knees, unwrapping pieces of foil and peering cautiously into **Tupperware** containers, when I came across an interesting product called a breakfast pizza and I examined it with a kind of **rueful** fondness, as you might regard an old photograph of yourself dressed in clothes that you cannot believe you ever thought were stylish. The breakfast pizza, you see, represented the last surviving **relic** of a bout of very serious retail foolishness on my part.

Some weeks ago I announced to my wife that I was going to the supermarket with her next time she went because the stuff she kept bringing home was – how can I put this? – not fully in the spirit of American eating. Here we were living in a paradise of junk food – the country that gave the world cheese in a spray can – and she kept bringing home healthy stuff like fresh broccoli and packets of **Ryvita**.

It was because she was English, of course. She didn't really understand the rich, **unrivalled** possibilities for greasiness and goo that the American diet offers. I longed for artificial bacon bits, melted cheese in a shade of yellow unknown to nature, and creamy chocolate fillings, sometimes all in the same product. I wanted food that squirts when you bite into it or plops onto your shirt front in such gross quantities that you have to rise carefully from the table and limbo over to the sink to clean yourself up.

Glossary

Gorgonzola: strong-smelling cheese
Tupperware: a brand of storage containers
rueful: sad, almost regretful
relic: leftover or remains
Ryvita: a brand of savoury cracker
unrivalled: nothing better; first class

AF 2 What country does Bryson say is 'the paradise of junk food'?

What reason is given for his wife not making the most of this paradise?

Find one example of food Bryson likes in each of paragraphs 1–3.

List three types of food that Bryson wishes his wife would buy from the supermarket in paragraph 4.

AF 3 Does Bryson really box up their fridge and send it to Atlanta Disease Control? If not, what does he really mean by this?

AF 4 What does the article gain from Bryson describing the Bryson fridge first (paragraphs 1–2) before moving on to the English wife's attempt to fill it differently (paragraph 3) followed by his rejection of this (paragraph 4)?

AF 5 Find the following phrases in the extract and comment on how they help to set the tone:

- 'I had a vague recollection of having glimpsed something furry'
- 'a bout of very serious retail foolishness'
- 'a shade of yellow unknown to nature'.

Write down at least one other phrase that helps to set the tone. Say how it does.

AF 6 Bill Bryson uses humour in this text to get across his point of view.

What are his feelings about American food? You should write about

- the way he uses humour
- the personal style of the text, using a first-person narrator ('I').

Remember to explain your answer using evidence from the text.

AF 7 Find examples in the text that tell you this is

a autobiographical writing

b about modern America.

How does the description of the American diet compare – or contrast – with your own? Give examples of each.

Under the silvering light of the cold, tall sky,

Where the stars are like glimmering ice and the moon rides high,

Bolted and locked since the war by long-dead hands,

Next to the shadowy church, the closed school stands.

A village school, in the grip of frost and the past,

Its classrooms airless as tombs, its corridors waste;

Behind boarded windows barely an insect crawls

On the spreading atlas that is staining ceiling and walls.

Here is the stillness of death. Listen hard as you can,

There's not one sound to be heard that is noisier than

The creeping of mould, or the crumbling of **masonry**

Into a fine floor-dust, soft and powdery.

Only deeper than silence, at the far end of listening,

Come the feet in the corridors, silver voices that ring

In the raftered hall, and outside, where the frost freezes hard,

Brittle laughter of children snowballing in the yard.

Glossary

masonry: stonework or brickwork
Brittle: easily broken; hard or sharp

AF 2 The school is not just shut for the holidays but has been permanently closed down. How do we know this? Find at least **two** phrases or lines that support this idea.

AF 3 What kind of atmosphere is created in this poem? You should use evidence from at least **two** of the four stanzas in your answer.

AF 4 The first three verses describe the look and feel of the building – the classrooms and corridors. What new, different description do we get in the final verse? What effect does this have coming at the end, rather than the start, of the poem?

AF 5 The poet uses several powerful images, such as 'the creeping of mould' (things we can see clearly in our mind), to describe the school and its surroundings. Choose **two** of these and explain why you think they work so well.

AF 6 What sort of effect does this poem have on you as a reader? How does it make you feel? Explain your thoughts and try to support them with evidence from the poem.

AF 7 How do you know this is a poem? Write about the particular features the text has that make this clear to you. Think about
- layout and organisation
- the use of sound and language
- what the text is about.

Scene 30

No-Man's-Land. They crawl on their bellies, snaking their way forward.

CHARLIE	*(whispering)* Stay close, Tommo.
TOMMO	*(whispering, to **Charlie**)* I'm not frightened, I'm excited. It's like we're out poaching again, Charlie.

They can hear the Germans: talking, laughter, a gramophone. They continue across No-Man's-Land, and drop down into the German trench.

TOMMO	*(whispering)* It's much deeper than ours, Charlie.
CHARLIE	*(whispering)* Wider too, and more solidly constructed.

They grip their rifles (mimed) and, bent double, move along the trench.

TOMMO	*(whispering)* We're making too much noise. Why has no-one heard us? Where are their sentries, for God's sake?

*Ahead **Captain Wilkes** waves them on (with his revolver). A flickering of light comes from ahead – that's where the voices and music are coming from. The trench floods with light as a German soldier emerges, shrugging on his coat. He spots the English soldiers – both sides freeze – then the German shrieks, turns and blunders back. Gunfire, then **Nipper** throws a grenade (mimed) and there is a blast which throws the English soldiers against the trench wall. Les has been shot through the head, dead.*

CHARLIE	It's Les. He's been shot. He's dead.
CAPTAIN WILKES	Grab the prisoner. Let's go!

The Germans all lie dead – except one, blood spattered, shaking.
Captain Wilkes *throws a coat over him and* ***Pete*** *bundles him out, the German whimpering. They scrabble their way along the trench, up over the top, and run. Then a flare goes up, seeming to catch them in broad daylight. They all throw themselves to the floor as the German machine guns and rifles open fire.*

TOMMO — I must think of Molly. If I'm going to die, I want her to be my last thought – sorry, Father, for what I did, I didn't mean to do it!

The flare dies.

CAPTAIN WILKES — On your feet!

They run off again and then another flare goes up – they dive into a crater as more intense gunfire and shelling starts, ***Charlie***, ***Tommo*** *and the German soldier huddled together.*

GERMAN SOLDIER — Du lieber Gott! Du lieber Gott!

TOMMO — *(to Charlie)* 'Gott'. They call God by the same name.

Captain Wilkes *is lying injured on the edge of the crater.*

CHARLIE — Captain Wilkes!

Captain Wilkes *doesn't respond so* ***Charlie*** *goes up the slope and turns him over.*

CAPTAIN WILKES — It's my legs. I can't seem to move my legs. I won't make it. I'm leaving it to you to get them all back, Peaceful, and the prisoner. Go on now.

CHARLIE — No sir. If one goes we all go. Isn't that right, lads?

They make their way across No-Man's-Land, ***Charlie*** *carrying the* ***Captain*** *on his back all the way. The stretcher bearers come for the* ***Captain***.

CAPTAIN WILKES	*(to Charlie)* Take my watch, Peaceful. You've given me more time on this earth.
CHARLIE	*(admiring the watch)* It's wonderful, sir. Ruddy wonderful.

*The **Captain** is stretchered off – the German is led away.*

GERMAN SOLDIER	Danke. Danke sehr.
NIPPER	Funny that. Seeing him so close to, you can hardly tell the difference.
TOMMO	Poor old Les.

AF 2 The British soldiers can hear noises from the German trench as they crawl towards it. List at least two things they hear.

AF 3 How does Tommo feel about the attack on the trenches at first, before they actually come across the German soldiers? Refer to evidence from the text to support your answer.

AF 4 Look at the stage directions – the text in italics. Explain what the purpose of these directions is. Think, in particular, how they might help an actor or director.

AF 5 Look at some of the short lines or phrases spoken by Captain Wilkes following the attack (from 'Grab the prisoner. Let's go!' to 'They dive into a crater as more intense gunfire and shelling starts'). How do you think an actor playing the Captain would speak these lines? Think about the purpose of the words or lines.

AF 6 Which of these statements best describes the writer's purpose in creating this scene? Explain your choice using at least two examples from the text.

- He wants to show how exciting war is.
- He wants to show the reality of war.
- He wants to advise young people about the best way to attack an enemy trench.

AF 7 This is a play written by a modern writer about the First World War, which took place between 1914 and 1918. At first it was seen as a big adventure and many young men signed up; later, with thousands dead, people realised how deadly and destructive it was for everyone involved.

Write a paragraph or two in which you explain

- what you have learned about the war from this brief extract
- whether you think the play presents the German soldiers sympathetically.

Support your views with evidence from the extract.

Rafael Nadal

By Serena Williams

I have never seen such tenacity, such ambition, such fight and such honor go into every shot as when I watch Rafael Nadal.

I want to be like him. The attitude he **exudes** the moment he walks out on the court is the attitude of a true champion. A champion whose desire to win is the same as the desire of a lion to eat. Stalking his prey with force and speed, Nadal, 22, has already become one of the game's all-time best.

What is so unusual about Rafa (which is what he likes to be called) is that unlike many of his fellow Spaniards, he can dominate on all surfaces. He has never lost a match on the French Open's clay, but he also has a Wimbledon title to his name, as well as one from the Australian Open. This year he's the only man able to go for a true Grand Slam.

What makes him so good? I think it's that he's the hardest worker. The last one to leave the court, the first to arrive. The one who falls asleep studying, the first to rise. It's not easy being a champion; you don't just wake up and — bam! — you're No. 1. It takes work, effort, desire, **dedication** — all qualities that Rafa has. I could be wrong, but I don't think I am far off.

Williams, whose memoir On the Line comes out in September, has won 20 Grand Slam titles

Glossary

exudes: oozes, gives out
dedication: commitment

AF 2   Serena Williams gives us a number of key pieces of factual information about Rafael Nadal's achievements as a tennis player. Note down at least two things you learn about these achievements.

AF 3   What single thing does Serena Williams say makes Rafael Nadal 'so good'?

AF 4   'Profiles' of famous people, like this, are organised in particular ways. But they are not identical. How does this writer make her personal opinion clear by returning to her original point in her conclusion?

AF 5   The profile uses a number of similes or metaphors to describe the tennis player. Write a sentence on each, explaining what these descriptions suggest.

'A champion whose desire to win is the same as the desire of a lion to eat.'

'The one who falls asleep studying, the first to rise.'

AF 6   Whose viewpoint is the text written from? What difference does this personal viewpoint make to the impact of the text on the reader?

AF 7   Texts in which the writer or speaker praises or describes someone else's qualities are quite common. This came from a magazine in which well-known people write about other people they admire.

- Can you think of any other kinds of texts that do this? (They can be spoken or written texts.)
- Choose one of the examples you thought of. Can you think of any obvious *difference* between your choice and the profiles here? (For example, mentioning the famous people someone has worked with might not suit a wedding day speech about the bride, but describing her good qualities might!)

Teacher Guide

Where the final task of the double-page section is substantial enough to provide a snapshot of students' progress, this has been marked as an **APP opportunity**.

Each double-page section ends with a **Check your progress** box. This offers a levelled checklist against which students can self- or peer-assess their final piece of writing from the **Development** or, occasionally, **Now you try it** section.

The end of chapter **Level Booster** is a less task-specific checklist of the skills students need to master to reach Level 4, 5 and 6. It can be used to help students see the level they are working at currently and to visualise what they need to do to make progress.

To the Teacher

The general aim of these books is the practical and everyday application of **Assessment for Learning (AfL)**: to ensure every child knows how they are doing and what they need to do to improve. The specific aim is to support **APP (Assessing Pupils' Progress)**: the 'periodic' view of progress by teacher and learner.

The books empower the student by modelling the essential skills needed at each level, and by allowing them to practise and then demonstrate independently what they know and can do across every reading and writing (APP) strand. They support the teacher by providing opportunities to gather and review secure evidence of progress in each **Assessment Focus (AF)**. Where appropriate (and especially at lower levels) the books facilitate teacher **scaffolding** of such learning and assessment.

The series offers exercises that we hope will not only help students add descriptive power and nuance to their vocabulary but also expand the grammatical constructions they can access and use: above all, the ability to write and read in sentences (paragraphs, texts) – to think consciously in complete thoughts.

We hope we can enrich how students read, recognising not just the texts they are decoding but also the contexts in which they read them. Our extracts cannot replace longer texts. The longer reading passages in Chapter 7 of our Reading books, with questions that cover all the AFs working together, are a crucial acknowledgement of this. Each AF is a provisional isolation of various emphases, to be practised and mastered before bringing it back to the real reading and writing of whole texts in which all these – suitably polished – skills can be applied.

Gareth Calway
Series Editor

1 Understand and respond to the key points in a text

Most students love horror stories, and Anthony Horowitz is one of the most popular authors, so this article should appeal.

Getting you thinking

Read the extract aloud to the class, using plenty of emphasis and humour where appropriate. Ask students for their initial reactions, including their reaction to Horowitz's claim that the writer of horror stories can never go far enough for children.

Ask students who they think Horowitz is writing this for, and what is the main point (or points) he is trying to get across. Then look at the three suggested statements. You could ask for a show of hands in support of each one.

How does it work?

Explain to students that the text was written to give advice to authors about how to write horror stories for children – they may well have deduced this for themselves. When Anthony Horowitz instructs the reader to 'Go into a classroom and talk to the children', it sounds as though he is talking to an adult audience.

There is evidence in the text to support the first two statements. Show students how to use the evidence they picked out from the text to write a full answer to question 2. For example:

> *The author makes the point very clearly that children like blood and gore when he says, 'They want the blood, the intestines, the knife cutting through the flesh'.*

or

> *Horowitz believes in letting readers imagine the horror for themselves, saying that often the most successful elements of horror stories are 'when the hand reaches for the door handle in the dark'. He says he advises children to keep their writing 'blood-free'.*

Students should have realised that Horowitz thinks horror stories don't have to be graphic and violent to be truly horrifying – and successful.

Now you try it

Either read the second extract to the class or ask for a volunteer to read it aloud. Discuss the two questions.

2 Comment on ideas from different parts of a text

This lesson transfers the focus to poetry, looking for key ideas in different parts of the text and linking them.

Getting you thinking

Depending on your class, either read the poem aloud to them or ask them to work in pairs as suggested. If they discuss the questions in pairs, take feedback from two or three pairs and discuss as a class.

How does it work?

As the title suggests, the poem is about a mother's strong and protective feelings towards her children. The whole poem expresses her love and concern for them.

Draw out with students that different sentiments are expressed in different parts of the poem:

- The first two stanzas include details that show the narrator hopes her children will not get physically or emotionally hurt by life: 'May you not / skin your knees. May you / not catch your fingers / in car doors. May / your hearts not break.'

- In the final stanza, the narrator wishes that her children may 'grow strong / to break / all the webs of my weaving'. This shows that she wants them one day to break out of the safety net she has made and be able to survive on their own.

Help students to see that, as readers, our attitude to the poem's narrator changes as we read the poem. At first, the mother seems almost over-protective, but we realise at the end that she wants her children to be strong and independent.

Now you try it

Read the poem *Nettles* to the class and ensure they understand all the vocabulary. The tasks are probably best discussed as a class. When discussing the final bullet point, ask students what other military imagery they can spot. Why do they think the writer has chosen to do this? What effect does it have?

Development

Students could write up their discussion and comparison of the two poems as a short essay or report.

3 Use quotations and refer to the text to support your ideas

This lesson encourages students to be selective and precise in their choice and use of quotations.

Getting you thinking

Allow students to read and discuss this advertisement in pairs. They should be able to pick out quotations without difficulty. You could also have a brief class discussion about the style of the writing, in particular the varied sentence lengths. Do they find this effective?

How does it work?

Start by taking feedback about the different quotations students have found. Write them up on the board and discuss which are the best quotations for each point.

Students may have come up with these quotations for the other points:

● **roomy** – 'fits family members of all sizes and their luggage', 'Spacious'

● **a good family car** – 'makes rear passengers of all ages feel as welcome as those in the front', 'fits your family's lifestyle – effortlessly', 'whether you're loading up at the supermarket, finding a place to park or simply heading off for a great day out'

● **powerful** – 'lively engine choices'.

Now you try it

Read through this advertisement with the students – it is also for a car but has a quite different style, to appeal to a different audience. Students should be able to spot suitable quotations to illustrate this.

Draw their attention to the final metaphor 'a true thoroughbred', which makes the car sound like a high-class racehorse.

Development

Students who finish early could pick a car of their choice and write some advertisement copy for it, clearly aimed at an appropriate audience.

4 Comment on the meaning of your quotations

This lesson centres on Vernon Scannell's poem 'A Case of Murder'.

Getting you thinking

Ask several different students to read this short poem extract aloud, then take feedback on which word they find the most disturbing. Students then discuss in pairs and write a short piece about it using the PEE structure (point, evidence, explanation) – either individually or with their partner if you think it is more appropriate.

How does it work?

Students now compare two different responses to the task they have just done. Draw out with them that the first response is better for several reasons.

The student focuses on a single word, 'buzzing'. He or she makes several intelligent comments about *how* it shows us that the boy finds the cat annoying, explaining how the word is usually used.

In the second response, the student quotes a whole line. Then, instead of focusing on an individual word and explaining its effect, the student makes a very general comment that just repeats the quotation. It would have been more effective to have explained that 'hated' is a really strong word, showing that the boy deeply disliked the cat.

Now you try it

Students now read a much longer section of the same poem, which contains the first short extract. Depending on your class, you may prefer to tackle this activity as a group discussion, to be sure students follow the development of the poem. Read the poem extract aloud to them first, with as much feeling as possible. Then model for them the analysis of one striking quotation, explaining what it tells us about the boy and how he feels. For instance, the fact that the author tells us he was 'only nine' perhaps makes us feel sympathetic towards the boy, to feel that he has been neglected, or cannot be held fully responsible for his actions.

Once students are confident with how this activity works, they could work individually or in pairs to select their quotations for the different stages of the poem and explain why they have chosen them.

Development

Before students read the last part of the poem, you could ask them how they think the poem will end. Read the ending to them and discuss reactions to it as a group. Elicit individual reactions to the poem. What do students think the image of the cat swelling and emerging from the cupboard means? Is it really coming back to take its revenge on the boy, or does it perhaps represent the boy's feelings of guilt?

Chapter 2 AF3 Deduce, infer or interpret information, events or ideas

1 Look closely at the meaning of individual words and phrases

This lesson uses newspaper articles about football to get students thinking about the power and precise meaning individual words and short phrases can have. Students will need access to a dictionary and a thesaurus later in the lesson.

Getting you thinking

Ask for a volunteer to read aloud the first short extract. Students might enjoy demonstrating what a 'slalom-like run into the penalty area' might look like. Ask them for other expressions that could be used to say the same thing, challenging them to come up with something equally powerful.

How does it work?

Use this to check that all students have understood the meaning of the two selected descriptions.

Now you try it

Again, you might find several volunteers to read aloud this second and longer football extract to the rest of the class. Check that all students are clear about the vocabulary used.

Use the example of 'sizzle' to explore with students what an individual word or phrase can add to the meaning of the text. Remind them that Rooney is sometimes seen as quite a 'fiery' character. What different meaning would be suggested by these alternative words and phrases?

Rooney began to sizzle...
Rooney started frying...
Rooney began to over-heat...

For example, 'started frying' suggests Rooney was sunbathing or actually frying something; it doesn't really fit the context. But what about the other two? Which one suggests he had a positive impact on the game? Which one might suggest he lost his temper?

Explain that words that have similar meanings are called **synonyms**. The key point is to understand why a writer might choose one word or phrase over another.

Development

The focus so far has all been on Manchester United's players – as was the case in the original article. Ask students now to consider the impression we are given of the Fulham team. Encourage them also to see how the omission of much significant description can also have an effect.

Some students could go on to write a piece of their own describing a sporting event – possibly a school team. They should do this as newspaper reporters, without showing bias.

Ask pairs to prepare a presentation to give to another pair, explaining how they think the writer wants us to feel about each team.

2 Develop your inferences and deductions across a text

Getting you thinking

Ask for a volunteer to read the first extract aloud. Then ask pairs of students to speculate about who and where the narrator might be. Take feedback and ask students to explain why they made the decision they did.

How does it work?

Allow students to read through this analysis in their pairs. Do they agree with it? Had they thought of any other points?

Now you try it

The next part of the extract tells us more about how the narrator is feeling, developing our understanding. Make sure students are all clear about the vocabulary and ask for any comments about the writing style and the effect produced. Then let them discuss in pairs what new information they can infer from this passage.

Development

In their pairs, or with two pairs working together, allow students to read the end of the extract. Once they have familiarised themselves with it, they should focus on the last sentence and feed back to the rest of the class.

Discuss with students how their comments about the narrator have changed or developed as you have looked at the evidence from across the text. Then read aloud the whole extract to them in one go, so that they see the cohesion and development. Ask them why they think the author saved the key detail – that the narrator is dying – until this point. What is the effect?

3 Use quotations effectively to support your inferences and deductions

Getting you thinking

Start by discussing which Roald Dahl books the students in the class have read. Are there any clear favourites? Ask those who like his books to try and explain why they enjoy them.

Then read to them the extract from a newspaper article. Do they agree with this analysis? Does it correspond to any of the explanations students may have given for liking Dahl's books?

Students should then read the two student answers to the question about Dahl's popularity. You could ask one student to read each one aloud.

How does it work?

Encourage students to see why the second answer is much better.

- The first one makes a very simple point but does not explain or justify it in any way, or provide any evidence to support it.

- The second answer has used PEE (point, evidence, explanation): the writer develops the **point** made and uses **evidence** to back it up. The answer selects relevant quotations from the text and **explains** the inferences made from these quotations. It also says what the reader has understood from the extract that isn't stated explicitly. In other words, the student has made some of his or her own inferences.

Now you try it

Read the different quotations from the article with students and make sure they understand all the vocabulary. Then ask them, individually or in pairs, to complete the table.

Development

Michael Rosen's personal description of meeting Roald Dahl sheds a different light on the author. Ask students what they learn about Dahl that is new.

Once they have written their paragraphs, students could work in pairs, comparing their paragraphs. Each could explain to the other how they have used the PEE pattern.

4 Read between the lines according to the purpose of a text

Students can sometimes find it difficult to infer meaning. Explain to them that it will help them to understand the *implied* meaning of a text if they are clear about the purpose of the text.

Getting you thinking

This gives students very clear examples of how you can interpret a text differently if you know who has written it and why they have written it. If someone is trying to sell something, that will always affect what they say and how they say it, especially if what they are trying to sell is not very appealing! You could ask students to say how they would describe something they wanted to sell, for instance, an old console game. How honest would they be?

You could show the class other examples of estate agent's descriptions.

Now you try it

Students focus on some of the particular words and phrases used in this longer estate agent's blurb. They should enjoy thinking about what each phrase might really mean.

Development

Encourage students to make the cottage sound as appealing as possible. To get them started, discuss as a class what could be changed or omitted, and brainstorm some phrases that could be used to imply subtly that the cottage is in a bad state. For example, they might not want to give so much detail about the outside toilet or the main road outside the house. 'Original features' or 'historic features' and 'close to traffic links' might imply the same things, but not state them explicitly to put off potential buyers.

Students who finish early could write an estate agent's description of another imagined property, then ask a partner to write a realistic description of the same property.

5 Make deductions about characters in fiction texts

This lesson applies students' understanding of inference to fiction writing, in particular to how it can be used to develop our understanding of character.

How does it work?

Explain to students that the key to success in understanding inference lies in close reading of the text. Reading closely helps us work out information about characters in a text. The following examples will help illustrate this:

- By reading the text closely we can find out that David's baby brother is a curious little guy. Even though he is still unsteady on his feet ('he wasn't what you'd call an expert'), he is energetic and keen to learn more about the world ('He toddled past his brother to the large open window').

- By looking at individual words and phrases, we can see that he is very determined. He puts in a 'great deal of effort' to getting up on the windowsill, as the verbs 'pulled', 'scrunched' and 'pushed' suggest.

Now you try it

Read the next section of the extract with the class. Ask students to look closely at the actual words used to describe what David says and does. There are a lot of verbs used in this passage. What is their effect?

Encourage students to use a verbal PEE approach in their answers – saying something they can infer about David's feelings, then quoting the words from the extract that imply this, then explaining how the words achieve it.

1 Recognise the genre of a text and understand reader expectations

Before referring students to the student pages, take a brief poll of the sort of books they like to read. Try to elicit as wide a list of genres as you can, perhaps adding one or two yourself.

Getting you thinking for

Ask students to identify the genres shown by the two book covers, then to list some of the features of this genre. Discuss the two blurbs with them, first asking them what the purpose of a blurb is. How important is it that the blurb gives a clear indication of the book's genre?

How does it work?

Explain to students that the actual look of the books (the image on the cover and the font used) should give a clue about their genre. If possible, show students the covers of other genres of book, by searching for them on Amazon.co.uk.

Discuss typical features of ghost or mystery stories with students. Ask them to share the features they had on their list. Do they include things like haunted houses, ghosts, unsolved murders, dark weather, sleepless nights and forbidden rooms?

Explain that in a ghost or mystery story, you would also expect tension to build up, with some 'cliff-hanger' moments. Maybe a character's life will be at risk or perhaps the ghost will harm the character somehow. You would expect to be scared when reading a ghost or mystery book!

Now you try it

Read the brief extract with the class and ask them what clues they can find as to the story's genre.

Explain that this is in fact a science-fiction story. They may have come up with other plausible ideas, such as action or adventure – this doesn't matter. Guide students to notice nouns like 'hovercars', 'satellites', 'aircrafts' and 'chemical glowsticks', which suggest a futuristic, hi-tech setting. Ask them to provide similar evidence for their own ideas.

Development

Lead a general discussion about science-fiction writing before students go on to do this activity. Ask students who like science fiction to talk about books they have read and what they liked about them. This will help those who are less familiar with the genre.

2 Identify structural features in a review

Getting you thinking

Ask students to think about reviews that they have read. What did they include? Ask students to write a list of the information they would expect to find and the order they would expect to find it in. For example, first you would be told the title...

Then ask them to read the review of *Twilight*.

How does it work?

Explain to students that, in order to comment on the structure and organisation of a text, you need to think about its purpose. The purpose of a review is to interest and entertain the reader, to tell the reader about the film, book or album and to make the writer's opinion clear.

The review of *Twilight* begins with a summary of the film and concludes with an opinion. Other reviews might start with an opinion and then go on to show how this opinion was formed.

Here:
- The first three paragraphs tell us what the film is about.
- The fourth paragraph tells us about the two main actors' performances, with some opinion.
- The fifth paragraph gives us some information about the origin of the film and how the director has adapted the book. It also states the reviewer's opinion.

Features such as a star rating, best line and best character add interest for the reader and allow them to see at a glance what the film is like and whether it's worth seeing.

Key information about the film's age rating and length are also included. These will also help people decide whether to see the film.

Now you try it

Based on the analysis of the *Twilight* review that you have taken them through, students should be able to go on to analyse the review of the album *Down to Earth*.

3 Understand the structure and presentation of a newspaper article

It would be helpful to bring in a selection of newspapers (local and national) to use in the Development section of this lesson.

Getting you thinking

Ask students to look at the newspaper article first without actually reading it. What do they notice? What do they think it will be about? Then give them 30 seconds to look at it in more detail and skim-read at least part of it. What more have they found out?

How does it work?

Go through the seven labelled presentational devices and make sure they are familiar with the vocabulary as well as with the function of each one.

1 This is the **headline** – a short, attention-grabbing statement that tells readers what the article is about and makes them want to know more.

2 Next comes the **by-line**, which tells us who wrote the article.

3 This is followed by a **lead paragraph** (or the 'nose'), which covers the basic information of the article. It usually addresses six questions: **Who**, **what**, **where**, **why**, **when** and **how**.

4 An **explanation** follows. Here, the writer includes other facts and specific details. Sometimes direct quotations from witnesses or relevant people are included.

5 Note that newspaper articles are written in **columns**, which make them easier to read.

6 The final section includes **additional information**, which might link the event or topic to something that has come before, so that we can see the story in its wider context.

7 **Pictures** may be included to make it more lively and eye-catching. **Captions** are sometimes included to explain what the pictures are about or offer a commentary on them.

Development

Students could go on to analyse the structure and presentation of other newspaper articles, either ones that they or you have brought in. They may be interested to compare the structure and presentation of articles from different newspapers and to think why they vary.

4 Discuss the effect of presentational devices in multi-modal texts

Students should be very familiar with different websites. Explain that like any other kind of text, the presentational features of a webpage will tell you a lot about its purpose and the audience it hopes to attract.

Getting you thinking

Students should discuss the MTV.co.uk webpage in pairs. If possible, allow students to visit the actual website – if the site is not accessible in school, they could do this at home and report back on the current site. Some may be able to take a screenshot of the current home page, which they can bring in to school.

Now you try it

This section is probably best worked on by students in pairs. Ask some to then feed back to the rest of the class.

Development

Encourage students to consider a range of different websites, likely to appeal to different target audiences and with different purposes.

5 Understand why writers choose different forms of poems

Getting you thinking

Read the poem aloud to the class or ask for one or two volunteers to read it. Ask students what they notice about the poem's structure. Do they like the poem?

Now you try it

Now read this very different poem about a girl's emotions. Who is the poem addressed to? Ask students for their reactions to the poem.

Then let students discuss the poem in pairs and try to analyse the way the poem is structured. Make sure they understand that sometimes a comparative *lack* of structure (in terms of regular form, metre and rhyme scheme) can also contribute to the form and meaning of a poem.

Development

Ask students to use their responses to the questions in 'Now you try it' to write a short piece about the form of the poem and its effect – how the form helps the writer communicate the poem's meaning.

Chapter 4 AF5 Explain and comment on writers' use of language, including grammatical and literary features at word and sentence level

1 Comment on metaphors

Students might already be familiar with metaphors, but check by asking them to suggest metaphors which you then write on the board.

Getting you thinking

Read the extract from a detective story, which is full of metaphors. Discuss what the first two mean.

How does it work?

The first metaphor is explained to students, and they are shown how they could comment on it. Ask them to explain the second metaphor (for instance, even the weather seems threatening; cold cannot literally 'stab' you) and how they might comment on it. For example:

This metaphor tells us that the cold felt like a sharp knife, that it was the type of cold that goes right through you.

Now you try it

Tell students that they will not be able to explain each of the metaphors fully without referring back to the text and how it was used in context. Once they have had a chance to write their explanations, take feedback and discuss why each one is appropriate.

2 Explore the tone and exact meaning of word choices

Getting you thinking

Read the extract aloud to the class, then ask students to read it to themselves slowly, trying to picture the scene in their mind's eye and making a note of the words and phrases they find most powerful. They can then compare ideas and discuss with their partner.

How does it work?

Students are taken through some of the more powerful and effective images in the extract.

Point out that the words also alliterate, which gives them extra impact, as the repeated 'b' and 's' sounds suggest the relentlessly beating rays of the sun.

Discuss with students how Larsen's word choices create an impression of intense, almost painful heat. For example:

- 'brutal' rather than 'shining' or 'kindly' suggests that the sun is remorseless and cruel
- 'blinding radiance' suggests that the sun is so bright it might damage your eyes

- 'buildings shuddered' suggests that even inanimate objects can't stand the heat, and also the shimmer of heat haze
- 'burning sidewalks' implies that the pavements are too hot to walk on
- 'seared … skins' implies that the skin of pedestrians is burnt or branded by the sun rather than 'warmed' or 'tanned' by it.

Now you try it

Students look closely at the powerful opening of the poem 'Ozymandias'. Explain that the poem contrasts the power of the long-dead pharaoh with that of the sculptor who made the statue, asking the reader to consider whose legacy has been more lasting.

Draw out with students that Shelley's specific vocabulary ('traveller' not 'bloke'; 'antique land' not 'abroad'; 'desert' rather than 'ground') all fix the image more carefully in our mind.

Development

Ask students to play with the language as they try replacing the underlined words with alternatives. They should say the new phrases to themselves so get a feel for the effect each change makes.

Finally, read the whole of Shelley's final version to the class, and enjoy it with them.

3 Comment on how and why authors vary sentence lengths

Getting you thinking

Briefly remind students of what a sentence needs to be grammatically correct (a subject and verb). Also remind them of the difference between a simple, compound and complex sentence. Then read the almost poetic extract, which contains several grammatically unusual sentences. What do they think the effect of this is?

Now you try it

As students read the extract aloud, in turn, encourage them to try and hear the rhythm of each sentence. Encourage students to link their analysis of sentence length to what is actually being described.

Draw their attention to the omens of death all around Torak from the 'ghostly skeletons' to the 'dying willowherb' and the 'three ravens'. Explain that these also contribute to the ominous mood.

Development

Students who finish early could attempt to write their own short descriptive paragraph using a variety of different sentences. Encourage them to be adventurous.

4 Identify formal and informal register

Getting you thinking

Remind students of the difference between informal and formal register by asking them what they might say to a visitor to their class who asked them to describe how they felt about school – and how they would answer the same question if asked by a new student in the class.

Then ask them to read the extract. You could try acting it out as a short play, with you playing the part of the narrator and students playing the parts of the two boys and Mr Rogers the head teacher.

Development

Give students different scenarios in which they either write informal and formal dialogue, or do

some formal and informal writing. They should make the contrast as great as they can. Possibilities include:

1 You write an e-mail or Facebook message to a friend, arranging to meet and go out this evening. You write a letter to your grandmother, thanking her for the money she sent for your birthday.

2 You and a friend discuss a film you have just seen or some music you like.

3 You go into a shop to ask if there might be any chance of a Saturday job.

5 Comment on the effect of past and present tense narration

Read the opening paragraph to this spread with the class. Ask them why the future tense is not often seen in narrative. On what occasions might it be seen (for example, in dialogue)? You could also ask them for additional examples of the past continuous tense. Can they explain when the past continuous would be used?

Getting you thinking

Students can read and discuss the two extracts in pairs. Make sure they understand all the vocabulary. Ask them to consider why the author chose each tense.

Now you try it

Remind students that, as a general rule, they should keep their tense consistent – in fact, changing tense is one of the things they should often check they have *not* done in a piece of writing. However, then go on to explain that it can also be very effective to vary tense within a paragraph, as in the extract from *Dracula*. The key is that it must be a conscious decision to achieve an effect, not a mistake!

Development

Once students have read and reflected on this later extract from *Dracula*, focus on the last paragraph. Ask them to think carefully about the difference between 'shall' and 'can' and to explain why both are used in this repeated question.

Chapter 5 AF6 Identify and comment on writers' purpose and viewpoints, and the overall effect of the text on the reader

1 Identify the writer's purpose in creating a text

Getting you thinking

Students will probably be quite familiar with the storyline of *Romeo and Juliet*, if not the play itself. Quickly recap the story with them so that it is fresh in their minds.

It would also be a good idea to talk about how identifying the writer's purpose can help in understanding a text. Remind students that a writer may have several purposes in mind when creating a text.

Look at the version of the play by Sonia Leong and ask students what they think the writer's purpose(s) might be in retelling the story of *Romeo and Juliet* in this way. Does it appeal to them more than the original Shakespeare play might do?

How does it work?

Students may have suggested some or all of the following purposes:

- One purpose of this graphic novel is to help teenage readers to understand *Romeo and Juliet* and to appreciate the story without the difficult language. Sonia Leong uses the popular Manga style of artwork to appeal to teenagers. By using this graphic novel format, combining words and images, she makes the story more accessible.

- The way the characters are presented and the change in the setting to modern-day Tokyo also makes the story more up-to-date and interesting for teenagers who might not want to read a play written over 400 years ago.

- Another purpose of the book is simply to retell the story in a new context. In this sense, the book will appeal not only to teenagers, but Shakespeare and Manga fans alike.

Now you try it

First, discuss briefly what the opening of any play or novel would try to do. Elicit from students that it would probably

- persuade the reader to continue reading (or grab the audience's attention)
- introduce the setting and context
- introduce the main characters or storyline, even if the characters themselves don't feature.

In pairs, students then discuss what information the Manga opening gives them, then go on to write their paragraph about the purpose of the text, backed up by evidence.

Development

When students have compared Shakespeare's 'Prologue' with Sonia Leong's opening, it would be useful to take brief feedback from around the class, to make sure all students are aware of the key points.

2 Identify the viewpoint of a text

Getting you thinking

In this lesson, students are asked to consider the importance of audience and viewpoint. They should find this leaflet straightforward to assess. Ask them for a quick first assessment of the likely audience. Some may initially feel the target audience is teenagers but, with a little reflection, they should see that it is in fact the parents of teenagers.

Now you try it

Look at the leaflet more closely with the class. Focus on the two sections highlighted in the book and discuss the questions as a class. Can they see how the viewpoint is actually more subtle than at first appeared?

Development

Encourage more able students to use evidence from other parts of the text. The complete leaflet is also available to download on the Parentline Plus website – www.parentlineplus.org.uk. Some students could be encouraged to look at other leaflets available to download and look in detail at the viewpoint.

3 Identify the effect a text has on the reader

Students will need a thesaurus in this lesson.

Getting you thinking

Start by brainstorming everything the class knows about Dracula. They may not realise that Dracula started out as a character in a novel written over 100 years ago. Explain that in the extract you are about to read the narrator is on his way to visit Dracula's castle.

Read the extract aloud to the class, building up the atmosphere, and check their understanding of the vocabulary. Ask for initial reactions to the extract: what effect does it have? Then allow students to discuss in pairs.

How does it work?

Take feedback from the pairs, then go on to read through this section with students. Had they discussed all these points? Did any pairs select other powerful phrases from the extract?

Make sure they are aware that there is no 'right' answer to this question – the effect of language is personal to different individuals. The key point is that students can explain why they find a piece of language powerful or effective.

Now you try it

Model an example or two so students can see how to fill in the table.

You may also want to draw students' attention to the structure of the extract and how it builds up tension as it goes on.

Development

Students can swap their work with a partner. Ask them to check whether their partner has explained fully every quotation and its effects.

4 Explain how the writer creates effects

Getting you thinking

Ask a student to read this one-sentence story aloud. Then ask the rest of the class how it makes them feel.

How does it work?

Point out to students that

- We aren't told the character's name, therefore we can imagine ourselves in the story.

- The semicolon and comma make you pause as you read. This creates more suspense for the reader.

- The use of the passive voice 'the matches were put' is subtly terrifying. It emphasises that we don't know who is doing this.

Now you try it

In this extract, the narrator arrives at the castle. Read the extract aloud to the class, or ask for volunteers to read it aloud. Check that all the vocabulary is understood, then allow students to work in pairs, if appropriate, to select descriptive language for the table and describe the effect of the language. They should work individually while writing their sentences, then share with their partner again.

Development

Students will probably be interested to compare a film version of these two scenes from the novel. Now that they have described the effects of Bram Stoker's language, they should have a clear image in their heads of what the castle looks like and what the atmosphere is.

Chapter 6 AF7 Relate texts to their social, cultural and historical traditions

1 Explore conventions in texts

Start by asking students what features they would expect to see in different types of text, for instance, comics, review articles, fairy stories. Ask students to discuss the headline in pairs and then join with another pair to share their ideas.

Getting you thinking

This lesson focuses on newspaper conventions. Ask students to discuss the headline in pairs and then join with another pair to share their ideas. Did they come up with the same ideas? How were their ideas for stories different depending on where the headline was?

How does it work?

This story actually appeared on the back page and is about the sprinter Christine Ohuruogo. If the headline was on the front page, the reader might think that the 'race plan' was about a government idea for racial equality, perhaps, or an election race.

Now you try it

Students can read this introduction to the actual article quietly to themselves. Then discuss as a class the conventions they can spot to do with the presentation of the article. Ask them why they think these conventions have been used.

Development

Students now consider the language of the article. Read through with the class the analysis of the phrase 'went out the window' and explain that a metaphor can be an **attention grabber** – a 'larger than life' way of writing. Sports pages are full of metaphors and dramatic language like this.

If students are struggling with describing what the other metaphors mean, ask them:

- Was Christine **actually** blind? If not, what does this phrase mean in terms of the race? (Tell them they will need to reread the first paragraph.)

- In what way was she in her 'own world'?

2 Understand how historical context affects the conventions, content and form of a text

So far, students have investigated conventions used in current texts. This lesson will help them to understand how those conventions can change over time, and the different forms of writing popular in different periods.

Getting you thinking

Having briefly considered current forms of writing that may or may not have existed 200 years ago, look at the ballad with students. Ask if any know what a ballad was and explain that ballads were sung – or recited – partly for entertainment but also as a means of passing news and stories on and keeping them alive. We take books and newspapers for granted these days but 200 years ago, few people could read and fewer still had access to books or magazines.

Read the ballad to the class, possibly asking for volunteers to read some of the verses, and ask for initial reactions to it.

Now you try it

Students discuss the ballad in pairs, starting with what they think it is about, then going on to look for the conventions of the text. Explain briefly that Australia was a penal colony and that prisoners had to endure a long and harsh boat journey to get there.

Development

Read the extract from the newspaper article to students and make sure they understand all the vocabulary. This gives them a different perspective on the same historical events. Explain that the extract from the *Sydney Cove Chronicle* is shaped very much by the context (the time, the place and the social setting) in which it was written. For example:

- It is clearly a 'local' paper with issues affecting its readers. Can they identify any examples which show this?

- The language/structure of the article shares some features with a modern report – it explains what **happened** ('Some expired in the boats') and the **situation now** ('convicts ... are stealing food'), but there are words, phrases and ideas that place it in its time.

- Ask students to find at least one word, phrase or sentence that they would not expect to see in a modern report of a disaster.

- Students can read the full article at http://www.familytreecircles.com/journal_6138.html

Now look at the following ballad with your students.

From The Ballad of Sir Patrick Spens

O loth, both, were our good Scots lords
To wet their cork-heel'd shoon,
But long ere all the play was play'd
They wet their hats aboon.

And many was the feather-bed
That fluttered on the foam;
And many was the good lord's son
That never more came home…

O lang, lang may the maidens sit
With their gold combs in their hair,
All waiting for their own dear loves,
For them they'll see nae mair.

Ballads were the news stories of the Middle Ages. This one describes a royal shipwreck in the reign of Alexander III of Scotland. His daughter Margaret is being escorted by a large party of nobles to Norway for her marriage to King Eric.

Ask students to compare and contrast how a shipwreck might be reported today. What conventions does this extract have in common with a news story? Ask them to rewrite it as a front page newspaper story.

Remember:

- the concentration on key details (gold combs = nobles, ladies)

- the tragic mood, life and death matters

- the 'picture' of genteel ladies waiting for the (drowned) lords to return. Is this like a modern newspaper photo?

3 Explain how context affects the way we read

Getting you thinking

Students become more familiar with what is meant by the context of a text by considering the famous poster of Lord Kitchener.

How does it work?

This was a **recruitment poster** commissioned by the British government to persuade people to enlist to fight in the First World War. It shows Lord Kitchener, the Secretary of State for War, encouraging men to join up.

We know it is a recruitment poster because of **text and context**. It combines big letters, pictures and a command, so it is a poster (text). It would have been displayed on 'official' walls in a country at war (context).

We are not in that war now so we read it differently – in a different **context**. It is still a poster, but we read it as history or art – displayed in classrooms or museums.

Now you try it

Students can compare modern-day recruitment posters and advertisements, seen in today's context. Encourage them to see how the huge difference in knowledge and awareness about the army's activities today compared with that in 1914 would affect how a recruitment advertisement would need to be prepared.

Development

Students may need to do some research about the beginning of the First World War in order to prepare this presentation effectively. This BBC website would be a good place to start:

http://www.bbc.co.uk/schools/worldwarone/

You could ask a small group of students to do the initial research and report their findings back to the rest of the class.

4 Explain how changing contexts affect the way texts are read

Getting you thinking

Look at the smoking advert with the class. Ask what cigarette advertisements they have seen and where, and make sure they know that such adverts are only permitted in very limited places (for instance, on Formula 1 cars) and are not allowed to actively encourage smoking. The 1930s advert is, of course, very different and comes from a time when no-one was really aware of the negative health effects of smoking.

Now you try it

Discuss as a class how the anti-smoking advert compares with the 1930s advert.

- Who is it aimed at?
- What devices are used to achieve its effect?

Then ask them to look back at the 1930s advert and decide whether they viewed it differently from how they think people would have viewed it at the time. Did they read it through 21st-century eyes, with 21st-century knowledge about smoking?

Development

Students will probably be very surprised to see some of the messages contained within this comic extract. Do they think this would be allowed now? Why, for example, is it very rare today to see a photo or read about a professional footballer smoking? They may be interested to know that some famous footballers in the past openly smoked a great deal.

Notes